INTERNATIONAL
LIGHT, SHAPE AND SOUND
SIGNALS

INTERNATIONAL
LIGHT, SHAPE AND SOUND SIGNALS

SECOND EDITION

D. A. Moore

HEINEMANN NEWNES

Heinemann Newnes
An imprint of Heinemann Professional Publishing
Halley Court, Jordan Hill, Oxford OX2 8EJ

OXFORD LONDON MELBOURNE AUCKLAND SINGAPORE
IBADAN NAIROBI GABORONE KINGSTON

First published by Stanford Maritime Ltd 1976
Reprinted 1981
Second edition 1982
Reprinted 1985, 1987
First published by Heinemann Professional Publishing 1989
Reprinted 1990

© D. A. Moore 1976, 1982

British Library Cataloguing in Publication Data
Moore, D. A.
    International light, shape and sound signals. – 2nd ed.
    1. Signal and signalling – Standards
    2. Aids to navigation – Standards
    I. Title
    623.89′4   VK381

ISBN 0 434 91310 3

Printed by BAS Printers Limited, Over Wallop, Hampshire

NOTE
The publishers, while exercising the greatest
care in compiling this publication, do not hold
themselves responsible for the consequences arising
from any inaccuracies therein.

CONTENTS

PREFACE TO THE FIRST EDITION

On October 20, 1972 the Inter-governmental Maritime Consultative Organization (IMCO) issued the final Act of the International Conference on Revision of the International Regulations for Preventing Collisions at Sea, 1972.

These new regulations, together with metrication, have brought about a number of changes in the positioning, ranges and types of lights and shapes required to be exhibited by vessels upon the high seas.

The purpose of this book is to illustrate the lights and shapes prescribed in the new rules and in order to do this effectively the book has been divided into three main sections:

Section 1 deals with the arcs of visibility, ranges, positioning and technical details of lights together with the sizes and positioning of shapes.

Section 2 illustrates Part C of the Regulations and wherever possible three aspects of the lights are shown and, where prescribed, the appropriate day signal. The fog signal for each case is also given.

Section 3 is in the form of a self-examiner where the reader is asked to identify the vessel exhibiting the lights or shapes shown.

This book should prove to be of value to those studying for their professional examinations, to all seafarers requiring a knowledge of the new Regulations and, in fact, to everyone who goes down to the sea in ships, whether large or small.

Finally, my sincere thanks go to those who assisted in the preparation and production of this book.

D. A. Moore, 1976

PREFACE TO THE SECOND EDITION

Since 1977 an IMCO Working Group has been active in considering proposals for changes to the 1972 Regulations and other matters related to the application of the Rules: this work has resulted in proposals for several amendments. In November 1981 the amendments were adopted by the IMCO Assembly and they came into force in July 1983. They have been incorporated in the text of the Rules which are quoted in this book.

With effect from May 1982 the name of IMCO was changed to the International Maritime Organization and the acronym IMO.

ACKNOWLEDGEMENT

The Publishers are indebted to A. N. Cockcroft, co-author of *Guide to the Collision Avoidance Rules*, for his assistance in the preparation of this new edition.

SECTION ONE

The definitions, visibility, positioning
and technical details of the lights,
shapes and sound signals required to be
carried by vessels upon the high seas.
Rules 3, 21 and 22
Annex I, II and III

GENERAL DEFINITIONS

RULE 3

For the purpose of these Rules, except where the context otherwise requires:

(a) The word 'vessel' includes every description of water craft, including non-displacement craft and seaplanes, used or capable of being used as a means of transportation on the water.

(b) The term 'power-driven vessel' means any vessel propelled by machinery.

(c) The term 'sailing vessel' means any vessel under sail provided that propelling machinery, if fitted, is not being used.

(d) The term 'vessel engaged in fishing' means any vessel fishing with nets, lines, trawls or other fishing apparatus which restrict manoeuvrability, but does not include a vessel fishing with trolling lines or other fishing apparatus which do not restrict manoeuvrability.

(e) The word 'seaplane' includes an aircraft designed to manoeuvre on the water.

(f) The term 'vessel not under command' means a vessel which through some exceptional circumstance is unable to manoeuvre as required by these Rules and is therefore unable to keep out of the way of another vessel.

(g) The term 'vessel restricted in her ability to manoeuvre' means a vessel which from the nature of her work is restricted in her ability to manoeuvre as required by these Rules and is therefore unable to keep out of the way of another vessel.

The term 'vessel restricted in her ability to manoeuvre' shall include but not be limited to:
(i) a vessel engaged in laying, servicing or picking up a navigation mark, submarine cable or pipeline;
(ii) a vessel engaged in dredging, surveying or underwater operations;
(iii) a vessel engaged in replenishment or transferring persons, provisions or cargo while underway;
(iv) a vessel engaged in the launching or recovery of aircraft;
(v) a vessel engaged in mine clearance operations;
(vi) a vessel engaged in a towing operation such as severely restricts the towing vessel and her tow in their ability to deviate from their course.

(h) The term 'vessel constrained by her draught' means a power-driven vessel which because of her draught in relation to the available depth and width of navigable water is severely restricted in her ability to deviate from the course she is following.

(i)   The word 'underway' means that a vessel is not at anchor, or made fast to the shore or aground.

(j)   The words 'length' and 'breadth' of a vessel means her length overall and greatest breadth.

(k)   Vessels shall be deemed to be in sight of one another only when one can be observed visually from the other.

(l)   The term 'restricted visibility' means any condition in which visibility is restricted by fog, mist, falling snow, heavy rain storms, sandstorms or any other similar causes.

DEFINITIONS WITH RESPECT TO LIGHTS

RULE 21

(a) 'Masthead light' means a white light placed over the fore and aft centreline of the vessel showing an unbroken light over an arc of the horizon of 225 degrees and so fixed as to show the light from right ahead to 22·5 degrees abaft the beam on either side of the vessel.

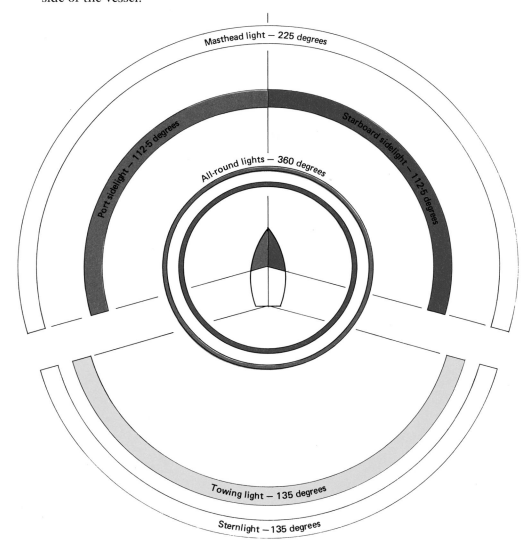

Arcs of lights as prescribed in the regulations

(b) 'Sidelights' means a green light on the starboard side and a red light on the port side each showing an unbroken light over an arc of the horizon of 112·5 degrees and so fixed as to show the light from right ahead to 22·5 degrees abaft the beam on its respective side. In a vessel of less than 20 metres in length the sidelights may be combined in one lantern carried on the fore and aft centreline of the vessel.

(c) 'Sternlight' means a white light placed as nearly as practicable at the stern showing an unbroken light over an arc of the horizon of 135 degrees and so fixed as to show the light 67·5 degrees from right aft on each side of the vessel.

(d) 'Towing light' means a yellow light having the same characteristics as the 'sternlight' defined in paragraph (c) of this Rule.

(e) 'All-round light' means a light showing an unbroken light over an arc of the horizon of 360 degrees.

(f) 'Flashing light' means a light flashing at regular intervals at a frequency of 120 flashes or more per minute.

VISIBILITY OF LIGHTS

RULE 22

The lights prescribed in these Rules shall have an intensity as specified in Section 8 of Annex 1 to these Regulations so as to be visible at the following minimum ranges:

(a)   In vessels of 50 metres or more in length:
    —a masthead light, 6 miles;
    —a sidelight, sternlight, towing light, 3 miles;
    —a white, red, green or yellow all-round light, 3 miles.

(b)   In vessels of 12 metres or more in length but less than 50 metres in length:
    —a masthead light, 5 miles; except that where the length of the vessel is less than 20 metres, 3 miles;
    —a sidelight, sternlight, towing light, 2 miles;
    —a white, red, green or yellow all-round light, 2 miles.

(c)   In vessels of less than 12 metres in length:
    —a masthead light, 2 miles;
    —a sidelight, 1 mile;
    —a sternlight, towing light, 2 miles;
    —a white, red, green or yellow all-round light, 2 miles.

(d)   In inconspicuous, partly submerged vessels or objects being towed:
    —a white all-round light, 3 miles.

POSITIONING AND TECHNICAL DETAILS OF LIGHTS AND SHAPES

ANNEX I

1. *Definition*

    The term 'height above the hull' means height above the uppermost continuous deck. This height shall be measured from the position vertically beneath the location of the light.

2. *Vertical positioning and spacing of lights*

    (a) On a power-driven vessel of 20 metres or more in length the masthead lights shall be placed as follows:

    (i) the forward masthead light, or if only one masthead light is carried, then that light, at a height above the hull of not less than 6 metres, and, if the breadth of the vessel exceeds 6 metres, then at a height above the hull not less than such breadth, so however that the light need not be placed at a greater height above the hull than 12 metres;

    (ii) when two masthead lights are carried then the after one shall be at least 4·5 metres vertically higher than the forward one.

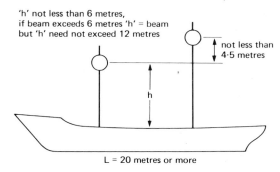

'h' not less than 6 metres,
if beam exceeds 6 metres 'h' = beam
but 'h' need not exceed 12 metres

not less than 4·5 metres

h

L = 20 metres or more

Vertical positioning of masthead lights

    (b) The vertical separation of masthead lights of power-driven vessels shall be such that in all normal conditions of trim the after light will be seen over and separate from the forward light at a distance of 1,000 metres from the stem when viewed from sea level.

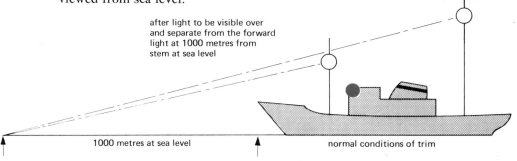

after light to be visible over
and separate from the forward
light at 1000 metres from
stem at sea level

1000 metres at sea level   normal conditions of trim

(c) The masthead light of a power-driven vessel of 12 metres but less than 20 metres in length shall be placed at a height above the gunwale of not less than 2·5 metres.

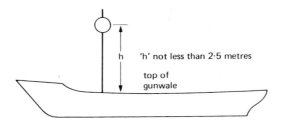

Length 12 metres or more but less than 20 metres

(d) A power-driven vessel of less than 12 metres in length may carry the uppermost light at a height of less than 2·5 metres above the gunwale. When however a masthead light is carried in addition to sidelights and a sternlight or the all-round light prescribed in Rule 23(c)(i) is carried in addition to sidelights, then such masthead light shall be carried at least 1 metre higher than the sidelights.

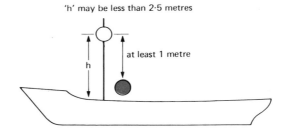

Where length is less than 12 metres

(e) One of the two or three masthead lights prescribed for a power-driven vessel when engaged in towing or pushing another vessel shall be placed in the same position as the forward masthead light or the after masthead light; provided that,

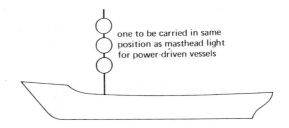

Location of mast lights for power-driven vessel engaged in towing or pushing

16

if carried on the aftermast, the lowest after masthead light shall be at least 4.5 metres vertically higher than the forward masthead light.

(f) (i) The masthead light or lights prescribed in Rule 23(a) shall be so placed as to be above and clear of all other lights and obstructions except as described in sub-paragraph (ii).

(ii) When it is impracticable to carry the all-round lights prescribed by Rule 27(b)(i) or Rule 28 below the masthead lights, they may be carried above the after masthead light(s), or vertically in between the forward masthead light(s) and after masthead light(s), provided that in the latter case the requirement of Section 3(c) of this Annex shall be complied with.

(g) The sidelights of a power-driven vessel shall be placed at a height above the hull not greater than three quarters of that of the forward masthead light. They shall not be so low as to be interfered with by decklights.

(h) The sidelights, if in a combined lantern and carried on a power-driven vessel of less than 20 metres in length, shall be placed not less than 1 metre below the masthead light.

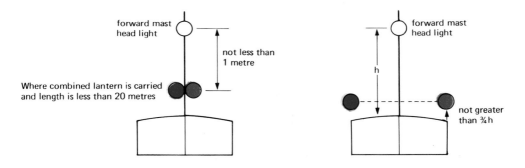

Vertical location of sidelights

(i) When the Rules prescribe two or three lights to be carried in a vertical line, they shall be spaced as follows:

(i) On a vessel of 20 metres in length or more such lights shall be spaced not less than 2 metres apart, and the lowest of these lights shall, except where a towing light is required, be placed at a height of not less than 4 metres above the hull;

(ii) on a vessel of less than 20 metres in length such lights shall be spaced not less than 1 metre apart and the lowest of these lights shall, except where a towing light is required, be placed at a height of not less than 2 metres above the gunwale;

(iii) where three lights are carried they shall be equally spaced.

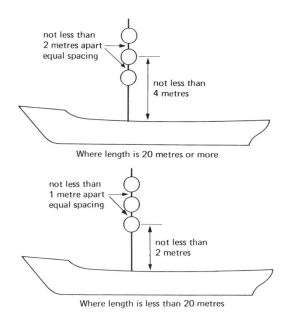

not less than
2 metres apart
equal spacing

not less than
4 metres

Where length is 20 metres or more

not less than
1 metre apart
equal spacing

not less than
2 metres

Where length is less than 20 metres

Spacing of lights carried in a vertical line

(j) The lower of the two all-round lights prescribed for a vessel when engaged in fishing shall be at a height above the sidelights not less than twice the distance between the two vertical lights.

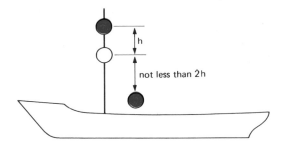

h

not less than 2h

Height of all-round lights for vessels engaged in fishing

(k) The forward anchor light, when two are carried, shall be not less than 4·5 metres above the after one. On a vessel of 50 metres or more in length this forward anchor light shall be placed at a height of not less than 6 metres above the hull.

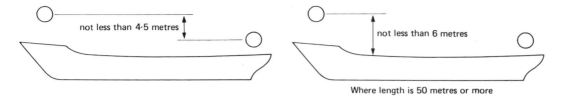

not less than 4·5 metres

not less than 6 metres

Where length is 50 metres or more

Anchor light spacing

3. *Horizontal positioning and spacing of lights*

  (a) When two masthead lights are prescribed for a power-driven vessel, the horizontal distance between them shall not be less than one half of the length of the vessel but need not be more than 100 metres. The forward light shall be placed not more than one quarter of the length of the vessel from the stem.

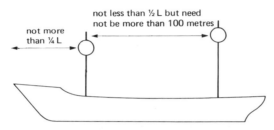

not more than ¼ L

not less than ½ L but need not be more than 100 metres

Horizontal spacing of masthead lights

  (b) On a power-driven vessel of 20 metres or more in length the sidelights shall not be placed in front of the forward masthead lights. They shall be placed at or near the side of the vessel.

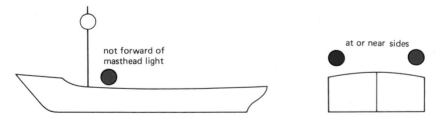

not forward of masthead light

at or near sides

Where length of vessel is 20 metres or more

  (c) When the lights prescribed in Rule 27(b)(i) or Rule 28 are placed vertically between the forward masthead light(s) and the after masthead light(s) these all-round lights shall be placed at a horizontal distance of not less than 2 metres from the fore and aft centreline of the vessel in the athwartship direction.

4. *Details of direction-indicating lights for fishing vessels, dredgers and vessels engaged in underwater operations*

(a) The light indicating the direction of the outlying gear from a vessel engaged in fishing as prescribed in Rule 26(c) (ii) shall be placed at a horizontal distance of not less than 2 metres and not more than 6 metres away from the two all-round red and white lights. This light shall be placed not higher than the all-round white light prescribed in Rule 26(c) (i) and not lower than the sidelights.

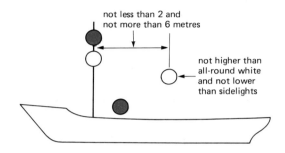

Location of direction light for fishing vessels

(b) The lights and shapes on a vessel engaged in dredging or underwater operations to indicate the obstructed side and/or the side on which it is safe to pass, as pre-scribed in Rule 27(d) (i) and (ii), shall be placed at the maximum horizontal distance, but in no case less than 2 metres, from the lights or shapes prescribed in Rule 27(b) (i) and (ii). In no case shall the upper of these lights or shapes be at a greater height than the lower of the three lights or shapes prescribed in Rule 27(b) (i) and (ii).

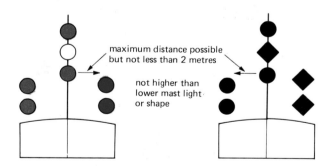

Location of dredging lights and shapes

5. *Screens for sidelights*

The sidelights of vessels of 20 metres or more in length shall be fitted with inboard screens painted matt black, and meeting the requirements of Section 9 of this Annex. With a combined lantern, using a single vertical filament and a very narrow division between the green and red sections, external screens need not be fitted.

6. *Shapes*

(a) Shapes shall be black and of the following sizes:

    (i)   a ball shall have a diameter of not less than 0·6 metre;

    (ii) a cone shall have a base diameter of not less than 0·6 metre and a height equal to its diameter;

    (iii) a cylinder shall have a diameter of at least 0·6 metre and a height of twice its diameter;

    (iv) a diamond shape shall consist of two cones as defined in (ii) above having a common base.

(b) The vertical distance between shapes shall be at least 1·5 metres.

(c) In vessel of less than 20 metres in length shapes of lesser dimensions but commensurate with the size of the vessel may be used and the distance apart may be correspondingly reduced.

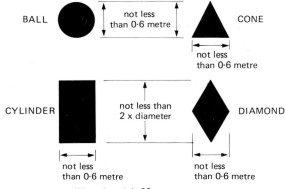

Where length is 20 metres or more

Sizes of shapes

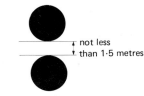

Where length is 20 metres or more

Vertical spacing of shapes

21

7. *Colour specification of lights*

The chromaticity of all navigation lights shall conform to the following standards, which lie within the boundaries of the area of the diagram specified for each colour by the International Commission on Illumination (CIE).

Author's note

Immediately following the above paragraph comes a list of coordinates denoting the boundaries of the four principal navigation light colours—white, green, red and yellow.

This section of the Annex dealing with the chromaticity of navigation lights is based on a chromaticity diagram by Hardy (reference: Principles of Optics by Hardy and Perrin, published by McGraw-Hill.).

An outline of the diagram is shown in the figure. Coordinate measurements are made with real primary coloured lights and then expressed in terms of imaginary primaries by means of a mathematical transformation. When the colour coordinates are determined in this manner, a colour can be plotted on the x-y chromaticity diagram.

The roughly triangular curve in the figure is the locus of the colours of the visible spectrum, i.e., colours produced by a single wavelength of light from the extreme red to the extreme violet. A straight line joining the ends of the visible spectrum closes the figure. Points representing all real colours lie within this boundary.

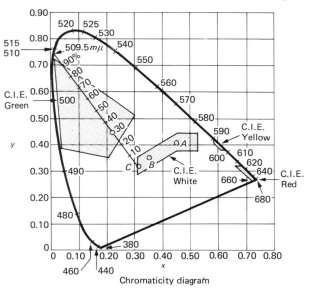

Chromaticity diagram

The points near the centre of the diagram marked A, B and C are white light standards representing approximately a bright light bulb, noon sunlight and average daylight, respectively.

There is no point in attempting to specify a colour for a navigation light exactly, and obviously some range of tolerance must be included. This is done in an objective way by specifying the coordinates on a chromaticity diagram which enclose an area of tolerance. The colour of an acceptable light would be represented by a point lying within this area.

8. *Intensity of lights*

(a) The minimum luminous intensity of lights shall be calculated by using the formula:

$$I = 3.43 \times 10^6 \times T \times D^2 \times K^{-D}$$

where I is luminous intensity in candelas under service conditions,

  T is threshold factor 2×10^{-7} lux,

  D is range of visibility (luminous range) of the light in nautical miles,

  K is atmospheric transmissivity.

For prescribed lights the value of K shall be 0.8, corresponding to a meteorological visibility of approximately 13 nautical miles.

(b) A selection of figures derived from the formula is given in the following table:

Range of visibility (luminous range) of light in nautical miles D	Luminous intensity of light in candelas for K=0.8 I
1	0.9
2	4.3
3	12
4	27
5	52
6	94

Note: The maximum luminous intensity of navigation lights should be limited to avoid undue glare. This shall not be achieved by a variable control of the luminous intensity.

9. *Horizontal sectors*

(a) (i) In the forward direction, sidelights as fitted on the vessel shall show the minimum required intensities. The intensities must decrease to reach practical cut-off between 1 degree and 3 degrees outside the prescribed sectors.

 (ii) For the sternlights and masthead lights and at 22.5 degrees abaft the beam for sidelights, the minimum required intensities shall be maintained over the arc of the horizon up to 5 degrees within the limits of the sectors prescribed in Rule 21. From 5 degrees within the prescribed sectors the intensity may decrease by 50 per cent up to the prescribed limits; it shall

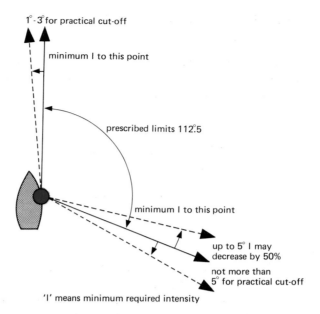

1°-3° for practical cut-off

minimum I to this point

prescribed limits 112°.5

minimum I to this point

up to 5° I may decrease by 50%

not more than 5° for practical cut-off

'I' means minimum required intensity

Horizontal sectors for electric sidelights

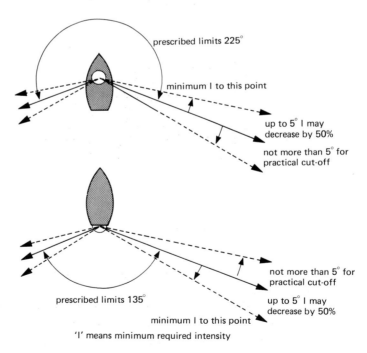

prescribed limits 225°

minimum I to this point

up to 5° I may decrease by 50%

not more than 5° for practical cut-off

not more than 5° for practical cut-off

up to 5° I may decrease by 50%

prescribed limits 135°

minimum I to this point

'I' means minimum required intensity

Horizontal sectors for electric masthead and sternlights

decrease steadily to reach practical cut-off at not more than 5 degrees outside the prescribed sectors.

(b) All-round lights shall be so located as not to be obscured by masts, topmasts or structures with angular sectors of more than 6 degrees, except anchor lights prescribed in Rule 30, which need not be placed at an impracticable height above the hull.

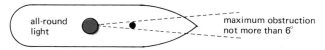

Maximum permitted obstruction for all-round lights

10. *Vertical sectors*

(a) The vertical sectors of electric lights as fitted, with the exception of lights on sailing vessels underway, shall ensure that:
   (i) at least the required minimum intensity is maintained at all angles from 5 degrees above to 5 degrees below the horizontal;
   (ii) at least 60 per cent of the required minimum intensity is maintained from 7·5 degrees above to 7·5 degrees below the horizontal.

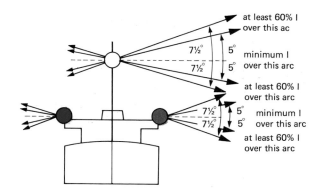

Vertical sectors for electric lights

(b) In the case of sailing vessels underway the vertical sectors of electric lights as fitted shall ensure that:
   (i) at least the required minimum intensity is maintained at all angles from 5 degrees above to 5 degrees below the horizontal;
   (ii) at least 50 per cent of the required minimum intensity is maintained from 25 degrees above to 25 degrees below the horizontal.

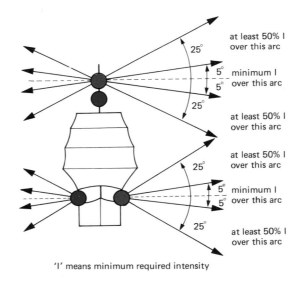

at least 50% I
over this arc

minimum I
over this arc

at least 50% I
over this arc

at least 50% I
over this arc

minimum I
over this arc

at least 50% I
over this arc

'I' means minimum required intensity

Vertical sectors for electric lights for sailing ships

(c)   In the case of lights other than electric these specifications shall be met as closely as possible.

11. *Intensity of non-electric lights*
Non-electric lights shall so far as practicable comply with the minimum intensities, as specified in the Table given in Section 8 of this Annex.

12. *Manoeuvring light*
Notwithstanding the provisions of paragraph 2(f) of this Annex the manoeuvring light described in Rule 34(b) shall be placed in the same fore and aft vertical plane as the masthead light or lights and, where practicable, at a minimum height of 2 metres vertically above the forward masthead light, provided that it shall be carried not less than 2 metres vertically above or below the after masthead light. On a vessel where only one masthead light is carried the manoeuvring light, if fitted, shall be carried where it can best be seen, not less than 2 metres vertically apart from the mast-head light.

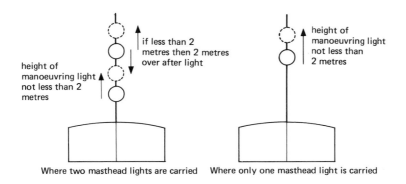

Where two masthead lights are carried   Where only one masthead light is carried

Location of manoeuvring light

13. *Approval*

The construction of lights and shapes and the installation of lights on board the vessel shall be to the satisfaction of the appropriate authority of the State whose flag the vessel is entitled to fly.

ADDITIONAL SIGNALS FOR FISHING VESSELS FISHING IN CLOSE PROXIMITY

ANNEX II

1. *General*

   The lights mentioned herein shall, if exhibited in pursuance of Rule 26(d), be placed where they can best be seen. They shall be at least 0·9 metre apart but at a lower level than lights prescribed in Rule 26(b) (i) and (c) (i). The lights shall be visible all round the horizon at a distance of at least 1 mile but at a lesser distance than the lights prescribed by these Rules for fishing vessels.

2. *Signals for trawlers*

   (a) Vessels when engaged in trawling, whether using demersal or pelagic gear, may exhibit:

      (i) when shooting their nets:
         two white lights in a vertical line;

      (ii) when hauling their nets:
         one white light over one red light in a vertical line;

      (iii) when the net has come fast upon an obstruction:
         two red lights in a vertical line.

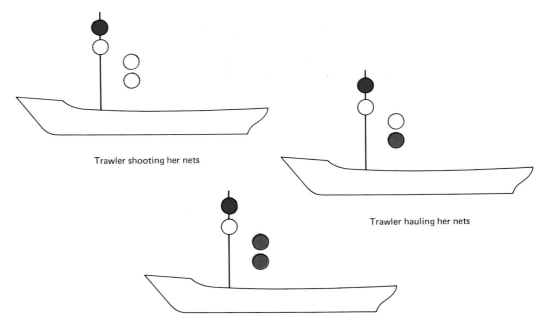

Trawler shooting her nets

Trawler hauling her nets

Trawler with nets fast on an obstruction

(b) Each vessel engaged in pair trawling may exhibit:
  (i) by night, a searchlight directed forward and in the direction of the other vessel of the pair;
  (ii) when shooting or hauling their nets or when their nets have come fast upon an obstruction, the lights prescribed in 2(a) above.

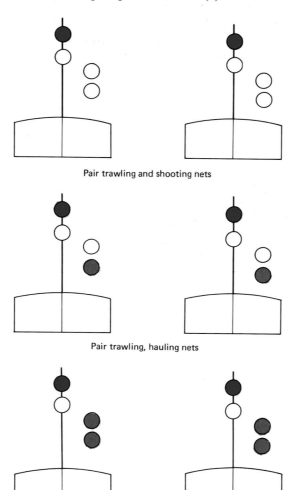

Pair trawling and shooting nets

Pair trawling, hauling nets

Pair trawling, nets fast on an obstruction

3. *Signals for purse seiners*

Vessels engaged in fishing with purse seine gear may exhibit two yellow lights in a vertical line. These lights shall flash alternately every second and with equal light and occultation duration. These lights may be exhibited only when the vessel is hampered by its fishing gear.

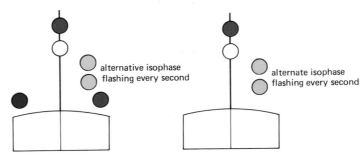

alternative isophase
flashing every second

alternate isophase
flashing every second

Purse seiner making way with her nets out   Purse seiner stopped with her nets out

TECHNICAL DETAILS OF SOUND SIGNAL APPLIANCES

ANNEX III

1. *Whistles*

   (a) Frequencies and range of audibility

   The fundamental frequency of the signal shall lie within the range 70–700 Hz. The range of audibility of the signal from a whistle shall be determined by those frequencies, which may include the fundamental and/or one or more higher frequencies, which lie within the range 180–700 Hz ($\pm$ 1 per cent) and which provide the sound pressure levels specified in paragraph 1(c) below.

   (b) Limits of fundamental frequencies

   To ensure a wide variety of whistle characteristics, the fundamental frequency of a whistle shall be between the following limits:

   (i)   70–200 Hz, for a vessel 200 metres or more in length;

   (ii) 130–350 Hz, for a vessel 75 metres but less than 200 metres in length;

   (iii) 250–700 Hz, for a vessel less than 75 metres in length.

   (c) Sound signal intensity and range of audibility

   A whistle fitted on a vessel shall provide, in the direction of maximum intensity of the whistle and at a distance of 1 metre from it, a sound pressure level in at least one $\frac{1}{3}$ octave band within the range of frequencies 180–700 Hz ($\pm$ 1 per cent) of not less than the appropriate figure given in the table below.

Length of vessel in metres	$\frac{1}{3}$ octave band level at 1 metre in dB referred to 2×10^{-5} N/m²	Audibility range in nautical miles
200 or more	143	2
75 but less than 200	138	1·5
20 but less than 75	130	1
less than 20	120	0·5

Author's note

Immediately following this table is a statement that this table is for information and quotes the ranges under ideal conditions. It warns that in practice the audible range of a whistle can be extremely variable and is dependent upon weather conditions.

   (d) Directional properties

   The sound pressure level of a directional whistle shall be not more than 4 dB below the prescribed sound pressure level on the axis at any direction in the horizontal plane within $\pm$ 45 degrees of the axis. The sound pressure level at any other direction in the horizontal plane shall be not more than 10 dB below the prescribed sound pressure level on the axis, so that the range in any direction will be at least half the range on the forward axis. The sound pressure level shall be measured in the $\frac{1}{3}$ octave band which determines the audibility range.

(e) Positioning of whistles
When a directional whistle is to be used as the only whistle on a vessel, it shall be installed with its maximum intensity directed straight ahead.
A whistle shall be placed as high as practicable on a vessel in order to reduce interception of the emitted sound by obstructions and also to minimize hearing damage risk to personnel. The sound pressure level of the vessel's own signal at listening posts shall not exceed 110 dB (A) and so far as practicable should not exceed 100 dB (A).

Author's note
An interesting point regarding the sound pressure levels is that 110 dB (A) is 10 times as great as 100 dB (A). The majority of experts agree that a sound pressure level of 120 dB (A) is the pain threshold while the level of 100 dB (A) is often referred to as the sound level of a boiler factory.
However it is interesting to note that at last some consideration is being paid to the noise problem and its often ill effects on personnel.

(f) Fitting of more than one whistle
If whistles are fitted at a distance apart of more than 100 metres, it shall be so arranged that they are not sounded simultaneously.

(g) Combined whistle systems
If due to the presence of obstructions the sound field of a single whistle or one of the whistles referred to in paragraph 1(f) above is likely to have a zone of greatly reduced signal level, it is recommended that a combined whistle system be fitted so as to overcome this reduction. For the purposes of the Rules a combined whistle system is to be regarded as a single whistle. The whistles of a combined system shall be located at a distance apart of not more than 100 metres and arranged to be sounded simultaneously. The frequency of any one whistle shall differ from those of the others by at least 10 Hz.

2. *Bell or gong*
(a) Intensity of signal
A bell or gong, or other device having similar sound characteristics shall produce a sound pressure level of not less than 110 dB at a distance of 1 metre from it.

(b) Construction
Bells and gongs shall be made of corrosion-resistant material and designed to give a clear tone. The diameter of the mouth of the bell shall be not less than 300 mm

for vessels of 20 metres or more in length, and shall be not less than 200 mm for vessels of 12 or more but of less than 20 metres in length. Where practicable, a power-driven striker is recommended to ensure constant force but manual operation shall be possible. The mass of the striker shall be not less than 3 per cent of the mass of the bell.

3. *Approval*

The construction of sound signal appliances, their performance and their installation on board the vessel shall be to the satisfaction of the appropriate authority of the State whose flag the vessel is entitled to fly.

SECTION TWO

The lights, shapes and sound signals prescribed for vessels upon the high seas.

Rules: 20, 23, 24, 25, 26, 27, 28, 29,
30, 31, 32, 33, 34, 35 and 36.

The distress signals contained in Rule 37, Annex IV and the Merchant Ship Search and Rescue Manual.

APPLICATION

RULE 20

(a) Rules in this Part shall be complied with in all weathers.

(b) The Rules concerning lights shall be complied with from sunset to sunrise, and during such times no other lights shall be exhibited, except such lights as cannot be mistaken for the lights specified in these Rules or do not impair their visibility or distinctive character, or interfere with the keeping of a proper look-out.

(c) The lights prescribed by these Rules shall, if carried, also be exhibited from sunrise to sunset in restricted visibility and may be exhibited in all other circumstances when it is deemed necessary.

(d) The Rules concerning shapes shall be complied with by day.

(e) The lights and shapes specified in these Rules shall comply with the provisions of Annex I to these Regulations.

POWER-DRIVEN VESSELS UNDER WAY

RULE 23

(a) A power-driven vessel underway shall exhibit:
  (i) a masthead light forward;
  (ii) a second masthead light abaft of and higher than the forward one; except that a vessel of less than 50 metres in length shall not be obliged to exhibit such light but may do so;
  (iii) sidelights;
  (iv) a sternlight.

Fog Signal *Rule 35(a) or (b)*
At intervals of not more than 2 minutes one prolonged blast when making way through the water and when underway but stopped two prolonged blasts with an interval of about 2 seconds between them.

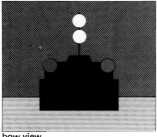
bow view

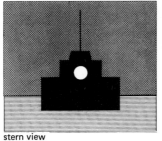
stern view

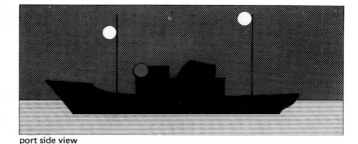
port side view

Power-driven vessel, 50 metres or more in length, under way.

bow view

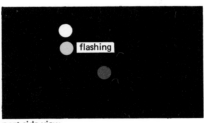

port side view

stern view

Power-driven vessel, less than 50 metres in length, under way

(b) An air-cushion vessel when operating in the non-displacement mode shall, in addition to the lights prescribed in paragraph (a) of this Rule, exhibit an all-round flashing yellow light.

Fog Signal   *Rule 35(a) or (b)*
As for a power-driven vessel underway.

bow view   port side view   stern view

An air-cushion vessel, less than 50 metres in length, under way

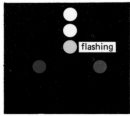
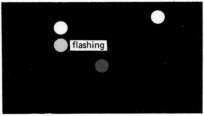

bow view   port side view   stern view

An air-cushion vessel, 50 metres or more in length, under way

(c) (i) A power-driven vessel of less than 12 metres in length may in lieu of the lights prescribed in paragraph (a) of this Rule exhibit an all-round white light and sidelights;

(ii) a power-driven vessel of less than 7 metres in length whose maximum speed does not exceed 7 knots may in lieu of the lights prescribed in paragraph (a) of this Rule exhibit an all-round white light and shall, if practicable, also exhibit sidelights;

(iii) the masthead light or all-round white light on a power-driven vessel of less than 12 metres in length may be displaced from the fore and aft centreline of the vessel if centreline fitting is not practicable, provided that the sidelights are combined in one lantern which shall be carried on the fore and aft centreline of the vessel or located as nearly as practicable in the same fore and aft line as the masthead light or the all-round white light.

Fog Signal *Rule 35 (a) or (b) or (i)*
As for a power-driven vessel underway but, if she does not make the prescribed signals, must make an efficient sound signal at intervals of not more than 2 minutes.

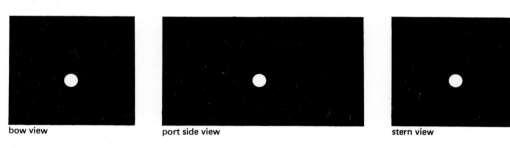

bow view   port side view   stern view

TOWING AND PUSHING

RULE 24

(a)   A power-driven vessel when towing shall exhibit:

    (i)   instead of the light prescribed in Rule 23(a) (i) or (a) (ii), two masthead lights in a vertical line. When the length of the tow, measuring from the stern of the towing vessel to the after end of the tow exceeds 200 metres, three such lights in a vertical line;

    (ii)   sidelights;

    (iii)   a sternlight;

    (iv)   a towing light in a vertical line above the sternlight;

    (v)   when the length of the tow exceeds 200 metres, a diamond shape where it can best be seen.

Fog Signal   *Rule 35*(c)

At intervals of not more than 2 minutes three blasts in succession, namely one prolonged followed by two short blasts. This would be followed immediately, if practicable, by the towed vessel sounding one prolonged followed by three short blasts, if manned.

bow view

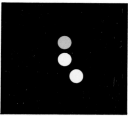

stern view

port side view

Power-driven vessel, less than 50 metres in length, towing with length of tow more than 200 metres

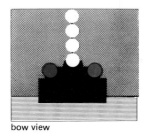
bow view

stern view

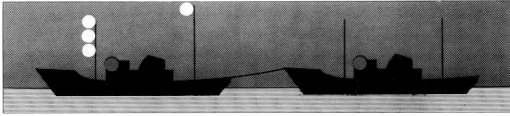
port side view

Power-driven vessel, 50 metres or more in length, towing with length of tow more than 200 metres

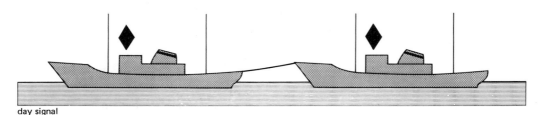
day signal

(b) When a pushing vessel and a vessel being pushed ahead are rigidly connected in a composite unit they shall be regarded as a power-driven vessel and exhibit the lights prescribed in Rule 23.

Fog Signal *Rule 35(f)*
As for a power-driven vessel underway.

(c) A power-driven vessel when pushing ahead or towing alongside, except in the case of a composite unit, shall exhibit:
   (i)   instead of the light prescribed in Rule 23(a)(i) or (a)(ii), two masthead lights in a vertical line;
   (ii) sidelights;
   (iii) a sternlight.

Fog Signal *Rule 35(c)*
At intervals of not more than 2 minutes one prolonged blast followed by two short blasts.

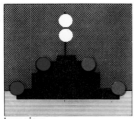

bow view

stern view

port side view

Power-driven vessel, less than 50 metres in length, engaged in pushing ahead

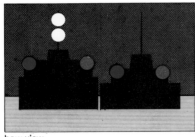

bow view

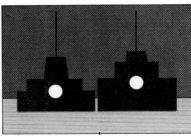

stern view

port side view

Power-driven vessel, less than 50 metres in length, engaged in towing alongside

(d)   A power-driven vessel to which paragraphs (a) or (c) of this Rule apply shall also comply with Rule 23(a) (ii).

Fog Signal   *Rule 35*(c)
At intervals of not more than 2 minutes one prolonged blast followed by two short blasts.

(e) A vessel or object being towed, other than those mentioned in paragraph (g) of this Rule, shall exhibit:
 (i) sidelights;
 (ii) a sternlight;
 (iii) where the length of the tow exceeds 200 metres, a diamond shape where it can best be seen.

(f) Provided that any number of vessels being towed alongside or pushed in a group shall be lighted as one vessel:
 (i) a vessel being pushed ahead, not being part of a composite unit, shall exhibit at the forward end, sidelights;
 (ii) a vessel being towed alongside shall exhibit a sternlight and at the forward end, sidelights.

Fog Signal   *Rule 35(e)*
If manned, the vessel towed or the last vessel of a multiple tow will sound at intervals of not more than 2 minutes four blasts, namely one prolonged followed by three short blasts and the signal should be given, if practicable, immediately after the signal given by the towing vessel.

Note   No fog signal is specified for a vessel being pushed nor for a vessel being towed alongside.

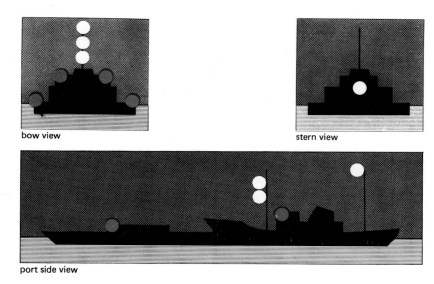

bow view

stern view

port side view

Power-driven vessel, 50 metres or more in length, engaged in pushing ahead

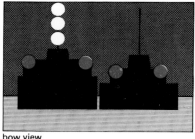
bow view

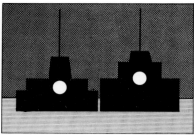
stern view

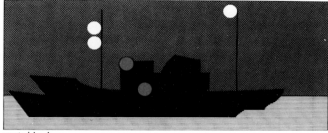
port side view

Power-driven vessel, 50 metres or more in length, engaged in towing alongside

(g) An inconspicuous, partly submerged vessel or object, or combination of such vessels or objects being towed, shall exhibit:

(i) if it is less than 25 metres in breadth, one all-round white light at or near the forward end and one at or near the after end except that dracones need not exhibit a light at or near the forward end;

(ii) if it is 25 metres or more in breadth, two additional all-round white lights at or near the extremities of its breadth;

(iii) if it exceeds 100 metres in length, additional all-round white lights between the lights prescribed in sub-paragraphs (i) and (ii) so that the distance between the lights shall not exceed 100 metres;

(iv) a diamond shape at or near the aftermost extremity of the last vessel or object being towed and if the length of the tow exceeds 200 metres an additional diamond shape where it can best be seen and located as far forward as is practicable.

SAILING VESSELS UNDERWAY AND VESSELS UNDER OARS

RULE 25

(a) A sailing vessel underway shall exhibit:
   (i)   sidelights;
   (ii) a sternlight.

Fog Signal   *Rule 35(c)*
At intervals of not more than 2 minutes one prolonged followed by two short blasts.

bow view   port side view   stern view

Sailing vessel underway showing only sidelights

(b) In a sailing vessel of less than 20 metres in length the lights prescribed in paragraph (a) of this Rule may be combined in one lantern carried at or near the top of the mast where it can best be seen.

Fog Signal   *Rule 35(c) or (i)*
As for a sailing vessel underway but, if she does not make the prescribed signals, must make an efficient sound signal at intervals of not more than 2 minutes.

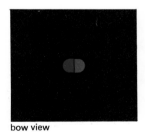 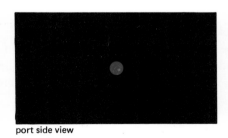 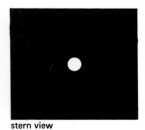

bow view   port side view   stern view

Sailing vessel, less than 20 metres in length, underway and showing combined lantern

(c) A sailing vessel underway may, in addition to the lights prescribed in paragraph (a) of this Rule, exhibit at or near the top of the mast, where they can best be seen, two all-round lights in a vertical line, the upper being red and the lower green, but these lights shall not be exhibited in conjunction with the combined lantern permitted by paragraph (b) of this Rule.

Fog Signal *Rule 35(c)*
As for a sailing vessel.

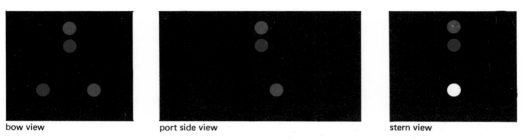

bow view port side view stern view

Sailing vessel underway showing sidelights and showing optional masthead lights

(d) (i) A sailing vessel of less than 7 metres in length shall, if practicable, exhibit the lights prescribed in paragraph (a) or (b) of this Rule, but if she does not, she shall have ready at hand an electric torch or lighted lantern showing a white light which shall be exhibited in sufficient time to prevent collision.

   (ii) A vessel under oars may exhibit the lights prescribed in this Rule for sailing vessels, but if she does not, she shall have ready at hand an electric torch or lighted lantern showing a white light which shall be exhibited in sufficient time to prevent collision.

Fog Signal *Rule 35(i)*
At intervals of not more than 2 minutes an efficient sound signal.

bow view port side view stern view

Sailing vessel, less than 7 metres in length; or a vessel under oars underway

(e) A vessel proceeding under sail when also being propelled by machinery shall exhibit forward where it can best be seen a conical shape, apex downwards.

Fog Signal *Rule 35(a) or (b) or (i)*
As for a power-driven vessel underway or making way or, if less than 12 metres in length, may give an efficient sound signals at intervals of not more than 2 minutes.

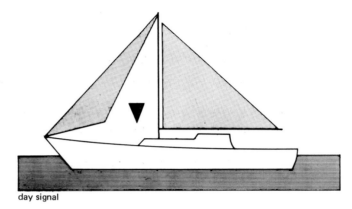

day signal

Vessel under sail and under power by day

FISHING VESSELS

RULE 26

(a) A vessel engaged in fishing, whether underway or at anchor, shall exhibit only the lights and shapes prescribed in this Rule.

(b) A vessel when engaged in trawling, by which is meant the dragging through the water of a dredge net or other apparatus used as a fishing appliance, shall exhibit:

    (i) two all-round lights in a vertical line, the upper being green and the lower white, or a shape consisting of two cones with their apexes together in a vertical line one above the other; a vessel of less than 20 metres in length may instead of this shape exhibit a basket;

    (ii) a masthead light abaft of and higher than the all-round green light; a vessel of less than 50 metres in length shall not be obliged to exhibit such a light but may do so;

    (iii) when making way through the water, in addition to the lights prescribed in this paragraph, sidelights and a sternlight.

Fog Signal   *Rule 35(c)*

At intervals of not more than 2 minutes one prolonged blast followed by two short blasts.

bow view

port side view

stern view

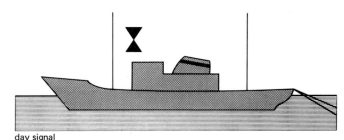

day signal

Vessel engaged in trawling and not making way through the water

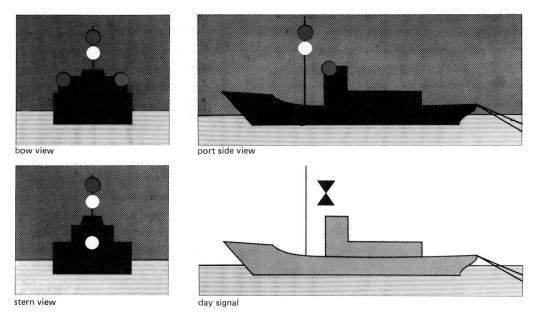

bow view

port side view

stern view

day signal

Vessel engaged in trawling, less than 50 metres in length and making way through the water

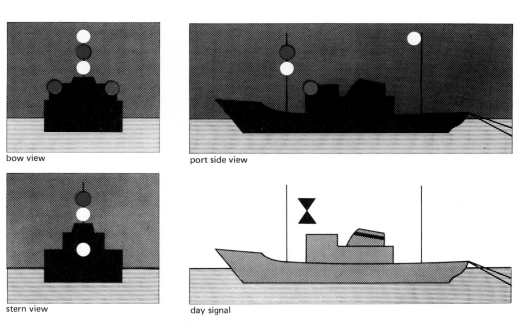

bow view

port side view

stern view

day signal

Vessel engaged in trawling, 50 metres or more in length and making way through the water

(c) A vessel engaged in fishing, other than trawling, shall exhibit:
  (i) two all-round lights in a vertical line, the upper being red and the lower white, or a shape consisting of two cones with their apexes together in a vertical line one above the other; a vessel of less than 20 metres in length may instead of this shape exhibit a basket;
  (ii) when there is outlying gear extending more than 150 metres horizontally from the vessel, an all-round white light or a cone apex upwards in the direction of the gear;
  (iii) when making way through the water, in addition to the lights prescribed in this paragraph, sidelights and a sternlight.

Fog Signal   *Rule 35(c)*
At intervals of not more than 2 minutes one prolonged blast followed by two short blasts.

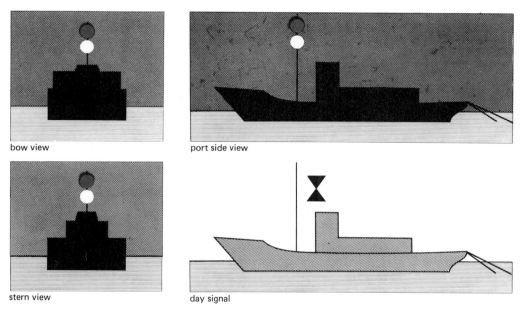

bow view

port side view

stern view

day signal

Vessel engaged in net fishing and not making way through the water

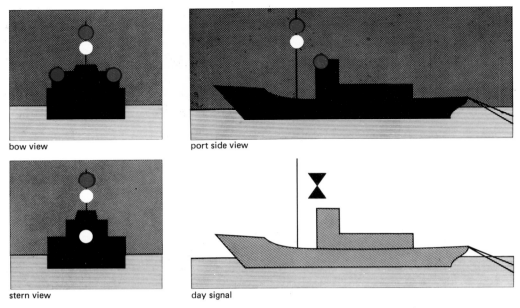

bow view

port side view

stern view

day signal

Vessel engaged in net fishing and making way through the water

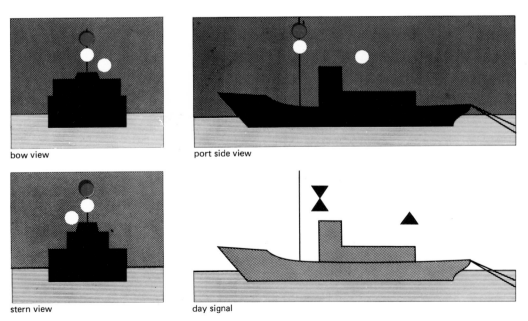

bow view

port side view

stern view

day signal

Vessel engaged in net fishing with nets extending more than 150 metres from the vessel
and not making way through the water

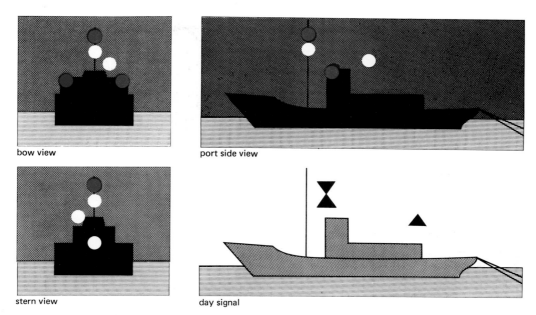

bow view

port side view

stern view

day signal

Vessel engaged in net fishing with nets extending more than 150 metres from the vessel
and making way through the water

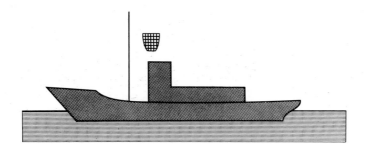

Optional day signal for any fishing vessel less than 20 metres in length

(d) A vessel engaged in fishing in close proximity to other vessels engaged in fishing may exhibit the additional signals described in Annex II to these Regulations.

Fog Signal   *Rule 35(c)*
At intervals of not more than 2 minutes one prolonged blast followed by two short blasts.

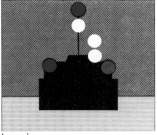

bow view

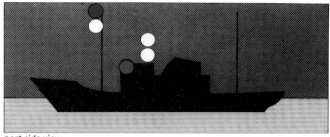

port side view

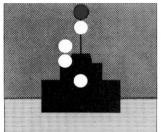

stern view

Vessel engaged in trawling, making way through the water and shooting the net

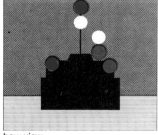

bow view

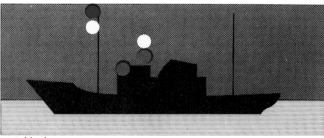

port side view

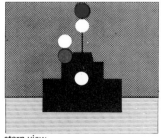

stern view

Vessel engaged in trawling, making way through the water and hauling the net

bow view

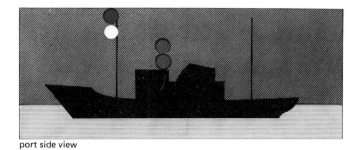

port side view

stern view

Vessel engaged in trawling with the net fast to an obstruction

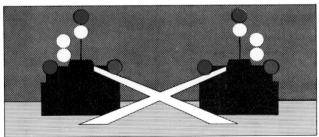

bow view

stern view

Vessels engaged in pair trawling, shooting their nets and using searchlights

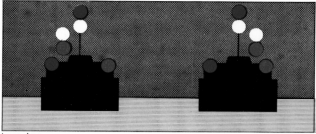

bow view

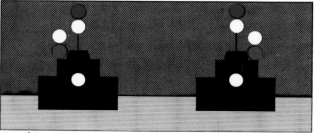

stern view

Vessels engaged in pair trawling and hauling their nets

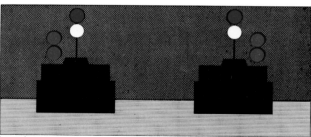

bow view

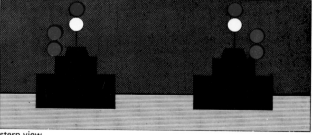

stern view

Vessels engaged in pair trawling with their nets fast to an obstruction

54

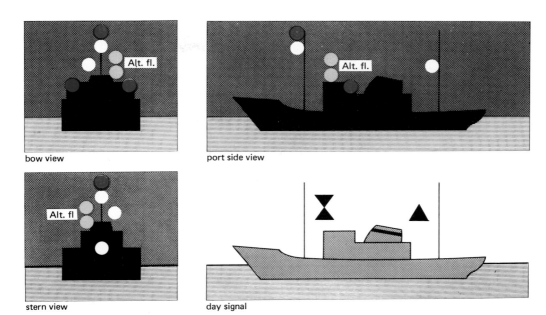

bow view

port side view

stern view

day signal

Vessel engaged in seine net fishing with nets extending more than 150 metres from the vessel

(e)　A vessel when not engaged in fishing shall not exhibit the lights or shapes prescribed in this Rule, but only those prescribed for a vessel of her length.

VESSELS NOT UNDER COMMAND OR RESTRICTED IN THEIR ABILITY TO MANOEUVRE

RULE 27

(a) A vessel not under command shall exhibit:

    (i)   two all-round red lights in a vertical line where they can best be seen;

    (ii) two balls or similar shapes in a vertical line where they can best be seen;

    (iii) when making way through the water, in addition to the lights prescribed in this paragraph, sidelights and a sternlight.

Fog Signal   *Rule 35(c)*

At intervals of not more than 2 minutes one prolonged blast followed by two short blasts.

bow view

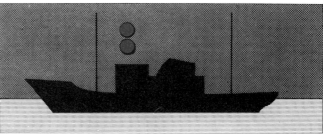

port side view

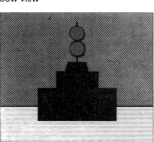

stern view

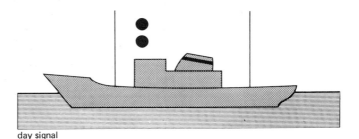

day signal

Vessel not under command and not making way through the water

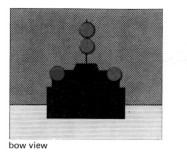

bow view

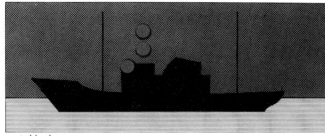

port side view

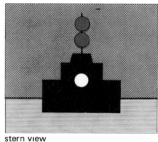

stern view

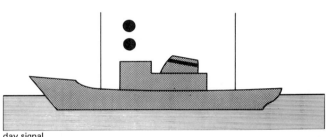

day signal

Vessel not under command and making way through the water.

(b) A vessel restricted in her ability to manoeuvre, except a vessel engaged in mine clearance operations, shall exhibit:

   (i) three all-round lights in a vertical line where they can best be seen. The highest and lowest of these lights shall be red and the middle light shall be white;

  (ii) three shapes in a vertical line where they can best be seen. The highest and lowest of these shapes shall be balls and the middle one a diamond;

 (iii) when making way through the water, masthead light or lights, sidelights and a sternlight, in addition to the lights prescribed in sub-paragraph (i);

 (iv) when at anchor, in addition to the lights or shapes prescribed in subparagraphs (i) and (ii), the light, lights or shape prescribed in Rule 30.

Fog Signal *Rule 35(c)*

At intervals of not more than 2 minutes one prolonged blast followed by two short blasts.

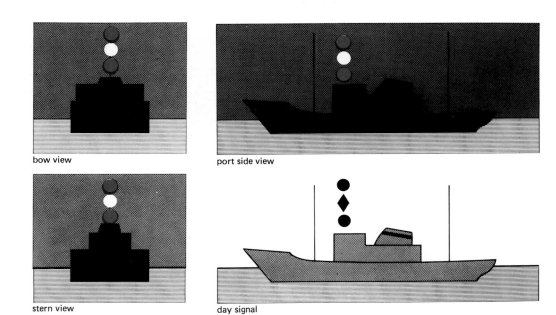

bow view

port side view

stern view

day signal

Vessel restricted in her ability to manoeuvre and not making way through the water

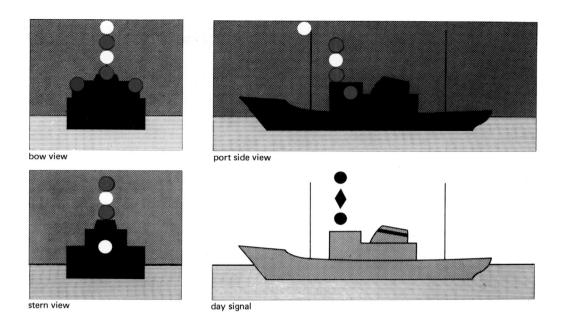

bow view

port side view

stern view

day signal

Vessel, less than 50 metres in length, restricted in her ability to manoeuvre and making way through the water

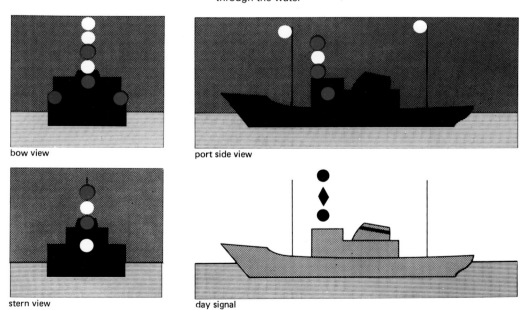

bow view

port side view

stern view

day signal

Vessel, 50 metres or more in length, restricted in her ability to manoeuvre and making way through the water

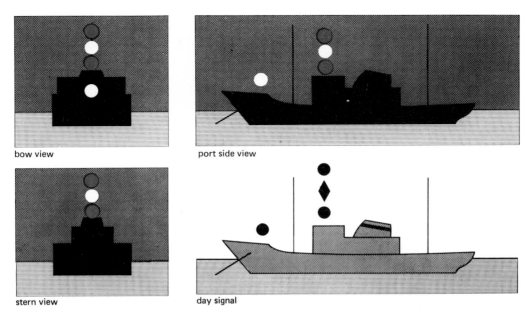

bow view

port side view

stern view

day signal

Vessel restricted in her ability to manoeuvre, less than 50 metres in length and at anchor.

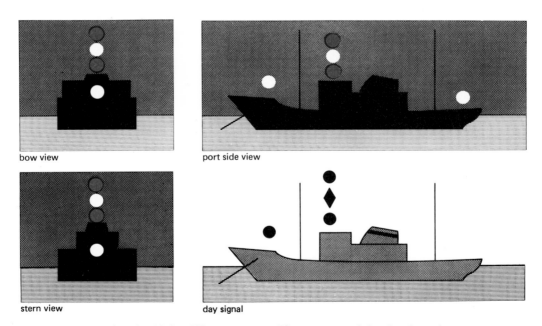

bow view

port side view

stern view

day signal

Vessel restricted in her ability to manoeuvre, 50 metres or more in length and at anchor

(c) A power-driven vessel engaged in a towing operation such as severely restricts the towing vessel and her tow in their ability to deviate from their course shall, in addition to the lights or shapes prescribed in Rule 24(a), exhibit the lights or shapes prescribed in sub-paragraphs (b)(i) and (ii) of this Rule.

Fog Signal *Rule 35(c)*
At intervals of not more than 2 minutes one prolonged blast followed by two short blasts.

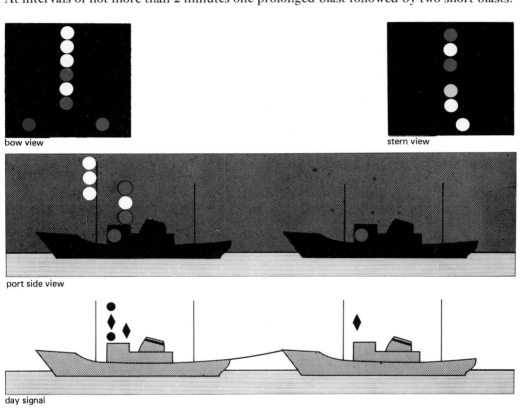

bow view

stern view

port side view

day signal

Power-driven vessel, less than 50 metres in length, towing and unable to deviate from her course

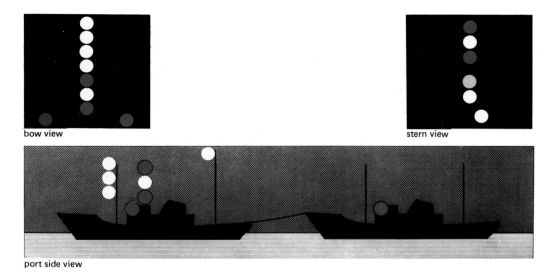

bow view

stern view

port side view

Power-driven vessel, 50 metres or more in length, towing and unable to deviate from her course

(d) A vessel engaged in dredging or underwater operations, when restricted in her ability to manoeuvre, shall exhibit the lights and shapes prescribed in sub-paragraphs (b) (i), (ii) and (iii) of this Rule and shall in addition, when an obstruction exists, exhibit:

(i) two all-round red lights or two balls in a vertical line to indicate the side on which the obstruction exists;

(ii) two all-round green lights or two diamonds in a vertical line to indicate the side on which another vessel may pass;

(iii) when at anchor, the lights or shapes prescribed in this paragraph instead of the lights or shapes prescribed in Rule 30.

Fog Signal   *Rule 35(c)*

At intervals of not more than 2 minutes one prolonged blast followed by two short blasts.

(e) Whenever the size of a vessel engaged in diving operations makes it impracticable to exhibit all lights and shapes prescribed in paragraph (d) of this Rule, the following shall be exhibited:

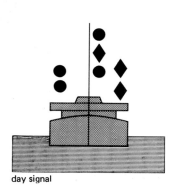

day signal

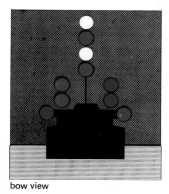

bow view

Vessel engaged in dredging or underwater operations and making way through the water

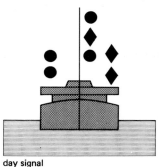

day signal

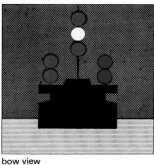

bow view

Vessel engaged in dredging or underwater operations and not making way through the water

(i) three all-round lights in a vertical line where they can best be seen. The highest and lowest of these lights shall be red and the middle light shall be white;

(ii) a rigid replica of the International Code flag 'A' not less than 1 metre in height. Measures shall be taken to ensure its all-round visibility.

Fog Signal *Rule 35(c) or (i)*

At intervals of not more than 2 minutes one prolonged blast followed by two short blasts, but if less than 12 metres in length may give an efficient sound signal at intervals of not more than 2 minutes.

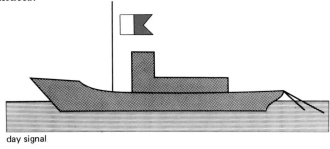

day signal

A small vessel engaged in diving operations

63

(f) A vessel engaged in mine clearance operations shall, in addition to the lights prescribed for a power-driven vessel in Rule 23 or for a vessel at anchor in Rule 30 as appropriate, exhibit three all-round green lights or three balls. One of these lights or shapes shall be exhibited near the foremast head and one at each end of the fore yard. These lights or shapes indicate that it is dangerous for another vessel to approach within 1,000 metres of the mine clearance vessel.

Fog Signal *Rule 35(c)*
At intervals of not more than 2 minutes one prolonged blast followed by two short blasts.

Author's note
While Rule 35 does not specifically state 'vessels engaged in mine clearance operations', this vessel is defined as a vessel restricted in her ability to manoeuvre in Rule 3 and the implication is that she would be governed by Rule 35(c).

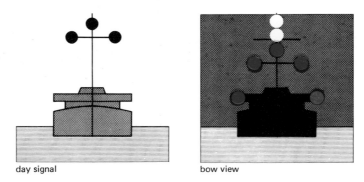

day signal   bow view

Vessel engaged in minesweeping operations

(g) Vessels of less than 12 metres in length, except those engaged in diving operations, shall not be required to exhibit the lights and shapes prescribed in this Rule.

(h) The signals prescribed in this Rule are not signals of vessels in distress and requiring assistance. Such signals are contained in Annex IV to these Regulations.

VESSELS CONSTRAINED BY THEIR DRAUGHT

RULE 28

A vessel constrained by her draught may, in addition to the lights prescribed for power-driven vessels in Rule 23, exhibit where they can best be seen three all-round red lights in a vertical line, or a cylinder.

Fog Signal *Rule 35(c)*

At intervals of not more than 2 minutes one prolonged followed by two short blasts.

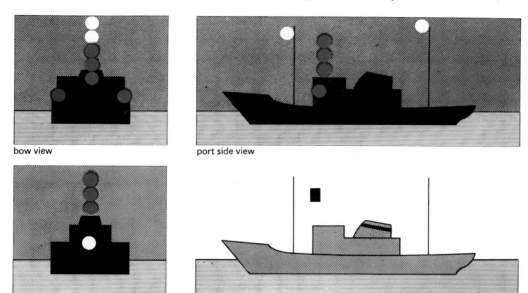

bow view

port side view

stern view

day signal

Power-driven vessel constrained by her draught

PILOT VESSELS

RULE 29

(a) A vessel engaged on pilotage duty shall exhibit:

    (i)   at or near the masthead, two all-round lights in a vertical line, the upper being white and the lower red;

    (ii) when underway, in addition, sidelights and a sternlight;

    (iii) when at anchor, in addition to the lights prescribed in sub-paragraph (i), the light, lights or shape prescribed in Rule 30 for vessels at anchor.

(b) A pilot vessel when not engaged on pilotage duty shall exhibit the lights or shapes prescribed for a similar vessel of her length.

Fog Signal   *Rule 35(a) or (b) or (i)*
As for a power-driven vessel underway, or making way, or at anchor and, in addition, *may* sound an identity signal consisting of four short blasts.

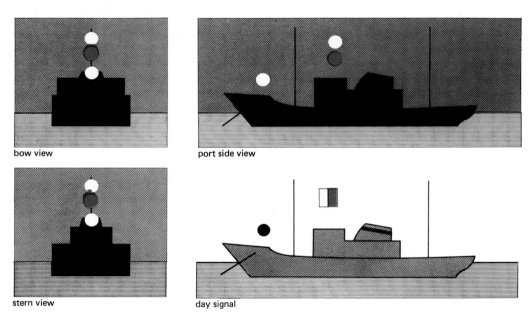

bow view

port side view

stern view

day signal

Pilot vessel, less than 50 metres in length, on pilotage duty and at anchor

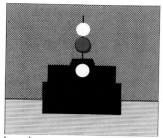

bow view

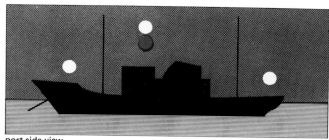

port side view

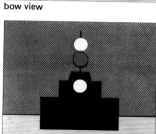

stern view

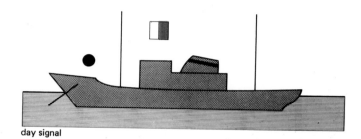

day signal

Pilot vessel, on pilotage duty and at anchor 50 metres or more in length

ANCHORED VESSELS AND VESSELS AGROUND

RULE 30
(a) A vessel at anchor shall exhibit where it can best be seen:
    (i)   in the fore part, an all-round white light or one ball;
    (ii) at or near the stern and at a lower level than the light prescribed in sub-paragraph (i), an all-round white light.

Fog Signal *Rule 35(g)*
At intervals of not more than one minute a rapid ringing of the bell for about 5 seconds. Where the vessel is 100 metres or more in length the bell is sounded in the forepart and the gong is sounded rapidly for about 5 seconds in the after part of the vessel immediately after the bell. In addition, a warning signal may be given consisting of one short, one prolonged and one short blast.

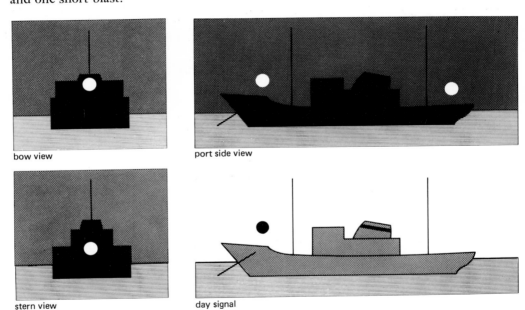

bow view   port side view

stern view   day signal

Vessel, 50 metres or more in length at anchor

(b) A vessel of less than 50 metres in length may exhibit an all-round white light where it can best be seen instead of the lights prescribed in paragraph (a) of this Rule

Fog Signal *Rule 35(g) or (i)*
As for any vessel at anchor but if less than 12 metres in length may, at intervals of not more than 2 minutes, give an efficient sound signal.

68

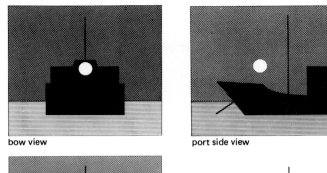

bow view

port side view

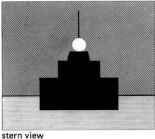
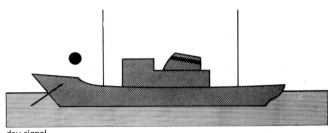

stern view

day signal

Vessel, less than 50 metres in length at anchor

(c) A vessel at anchor may, and a vessel of 100 metres or more in length shall, also use the available working or equivalent lights to illuminate her decks.

(d) A vessel aground shall exhibit the lights prescribed in paragraph (a) or (b) of this Rule and in addition, where they can best be seen:
(i)   two all–round red lights in a vertical line;
(ii) three balls in a vertical line.

Fog Signal *Rule 35(h) with reference to paragraph (g).*
The fog signal for a vessel at anchor and in addition, gives three separate and distinct strokes on the bell immediately before and after the rapid ringing of the bell.
In addition the vessel aground may sound an appropriate whistle signal.

(e) A vessel of less than 7 metres in length, when at anchor, not in or near a narrow channel, fairway or anchorage, or where other vessels normally navigate, shall not be required to exhibit the lights or shapes prescribed in paragraphs (a) and (b) of this Rule.

(f) A vessel of less than 12 metres in length, when aground, shall not be required to exhibit the lights or shapes prescribed in sub-paragraphs (d) (i) and (ii) of this Rule.

bow view

port side view

stern view

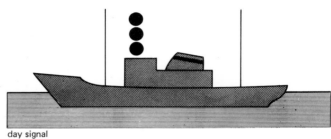

day signal

Vessel, less than 50 metres in length aground

bow view

port side view

stern view

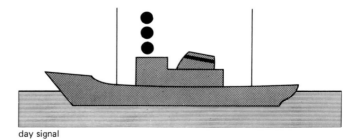

day signal

Vessel, 50 metres or more in length aground

SEAPLANES

RULE 31
Where it is impracticable for a seaplane to exhibit lights and shapes of the characteristics or in the positions prescribed in the Rules of this Part she shall exhibit lights and shapes as closely similar in characteristics and position as is possible.

Fog Signal *Rule 35(a) or (b) or (c)*
As for a power-driven vessel underway or making way or at anchor.

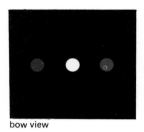

bow view

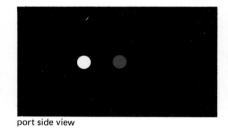

port side view

stern view

Possible distribution of a seaplane's lights

SOUND AND LIGHT SIGNALS

DEFINITIONS

RULE 32

(a) The word 'whistle' means any sound signalling appliance capable of producing the prescribed blasts and which complies with the specifications in Annex III to these Regulations.

(b) The term 'short blast' means a blast of about one second's duration.

(c) The term 'prolonged blast' means a blast of from four to six seconds' duration.

EQUIPMENT FOR SOUND SIGNALS

RULE 33

(a) A vessel of 12 metres or more in length shall be provided with a whistle and a bell and a vessel of 100 metres or more in length shall, in addition, be provided with a gong, the tone and sound of which cannot be confused with that of the bell. The whistle, bell and gong shall comply with the specifications in Annex III to these Regulations. The bell or gong or both may be replaced by other equipment having the same respective sound characteristics, provided that manual sounding of the prescribed signals shall always be possible.

(b) A vessel of less than 12 metres in length shall not be obliged to carry the sound signalling appliances prescribed in paragraph (a) of this Rule but if she does not, she shall be provided with some other means of making an efficient sound signal.

MANOEUVRING AND WARNING SIGNALS
RULE 34
(a) When vessels are in sight of one another, a power-driven vessel underway, when manoeuvring as authorised or required by these Rules, shall indicate that manoeuvre by the following signals on her whistle:

— one short blast to mean 'I am altering my course to starboard';

— two short blasts to mean 'I am altering my course to port';

— three short blasts to mean 'I am operating astern propulsion'.

(b) Any vessel may supplement the whistle signals prescribed in paragraph (a) of this Rule by light signals, repeated as appropriate, while the manoeuvre is being carried out:

(i) these light signals shall have the following significance:

— one flash to mean 'I am altering my course to starboard';

— two flashes to mean 'I am altering my course to port';

— three flashes to mean 'I am operating astern propulsion';

(ii) the duration of each flash shall be about one second, the interval between flashes shall be about one second, and the interval between successive signals shall be not less than ten seconds;

(iii) the light used for this signal shall, if fitted, be an all-round white light, visible at a minimum range of 5 miles, and shall comply with the provisions of Annex I to these Regulations.

(c) When in sight of one another in a narrow channel or fairway:

(i) a vessel intending to overtake another shall in compliance with Rule 9(e) (i) indicate her intention by the following signals on her whistle:

— two prolonged blasts followed by one short blast to mean 'I intend to overtake you on your starboard side';

— two prolonged blasts followed by two short blasts to mean 'I intend to overtake you on your port side';

(ii) the vessel about to be overtaken when acting in accordance with Rule 9(e) (i) shall indicate her agreement by the following signal on her whistle:

— one prolonged, one short, one prolonged and one short blast, in that order.

(d) When vessels are in sight of one another and approaching each other and from any cause either vessel fails to understand the intentions or actions of the other, or is in doubt whether sufficient action is being taken by the other to avoid collision, the vessel in doubt shall immediately indicate such doubt by giving at least five short and rapid blasts on the whistle. Such signal may be supplemented by a light signal of at least five short and rapid flashes.

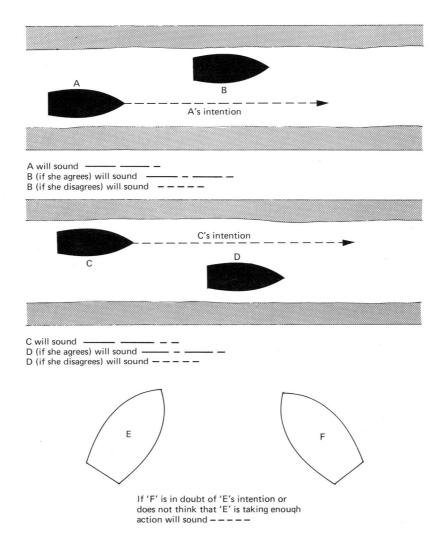

A will sound ——— ——— –
B (if she agrees) will sound ——— – ——— –
B (if she disagrees) will sound – – – – –

C will sound ——— ——— – –
D (if she agrees) will sound ——— – ——— –
D (if she disagrees) will sound – – – – –

If 'F' is in doubt of 'E's intention or
does not think that 'E' is taking enough
action will sound – – – – –

(e)   A vessel nearing a bend or an area of a channel or fairway where other vessels may be
      obscured by an intervening obstruction shall sound one prolonged blast. Such signal
      shall be answered with a prolonged blast by any approaching vessel that may be within
      hearing around the bend or behind the intervening obstruction.

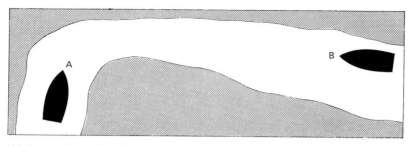

'A'   (nearing bend and unable to see beyond)
        would sound one prolonged blast

'B'   (if in range of audibility) would reply
        with one prolonged blast

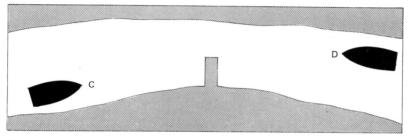

'C'   (nearing jetty and unable to see beyond)
        would sound one prolonged blast

'D'   (if in range of audibility) would reply
        with one prolonged blast

(f)   If whistles are fitted on a vessel at a distance apart of more than 100 metres, one whistle only shall be used for giving manoeuvring and warning signals.

SOUND SIGNALS IN RESTRICTED VISIBILITY

RULE 35

In or near an area of restricted visibility, whether by day or night, the signals prescribed in this Rule shall be used as follows:

(a) A power-driven vessel making way through the water shall sound at intervals of not more than 2 minutes one prolonged blast.

(b) A power-driven vessel under way but stopped and making no way through the water shall sound at intervals of not more than 2 minutes two prolonged blasts in succession with an interval of about 2 seconds between them.

(c) A vessel not under command, a vessel restricted in her ability to manoeuvre, a vessel constrained by her draught, a sailing vessel, a vessel engaged in fishing and a vessel engaged in towing or pushing another vessel shall, instead of the signals prescribed in paragraphs (a) or (b) of this Rule, sound at intervals of not more than 2 minutes three blasts in succession, namely one prolonged followed by two short blasts.

(d) A vessel engaged in fishing, when at anchor, and a vessel restricted in her ability to manoeuvre when carrying out her work at anchor, shall instead of the signals prescribed in paragraph (g) of this Rule sound the signal prescribed in paragraph (c) of this Rule.

(e) A vessel towed or if more than one vessel is towed the last vessel of the tow, if manned, shall at intervals of not more than 2 minutes sound four blasts in succession, namely one prolonged followed by three short blasts. When practicable, this signal shall be made immediately after the signal made by the towing vessel.

(f) When a pushing vessel and a vessel being pushed ahead are rigidly connected in a composite unit they shall be regarded as a power-driven vessel and shall give the signals prescribed in paragraphs (a) or (b) of this Rule.

(g) A vessel at anchor shall at intervals of not more than one minute ring the bell rapidly for about 5 seconds. In a vessel of 100 metres or more in length the bell shall be sounded in the forepart of the vessel and immediately after the ringing of the bell the gong shall be sounded rapidly for about 5 seconds in the after part of the vessel. A vessel at anchor may in addition sound three blasts in succession, namely one short, one prolonged and one short blast, to give warning of her position and of the possibility of collision to an approaching vessel.

(h) A vessel aground shall give the bell signal and if required the gong signal prescribed in paragraph (g) of this Rule and shall, in addition, give three separate and distinct strokes on the bell immediately before and after the rapid ringing of the bell. A vessel aground may in addition sound an appropriate whistle signal.

(i)   A vessel of less than 12 metres in length shall not be obliged to give the above-mentioned signals but, if she does not, shall make some other efficient sound signal at intervals of not more than 2 minutes.

(j)   A pilot vessel when engaged on pilotage duty may in addition to the signals prescribed in paragraphs (a), (b) or (g) of this Rule sound an identity signal consisting of four short blasts.

RULE 36

If necessary to attract the attention of another vessel any vessel may make light or sound signals that cannot be mistaken for any signal authorised elsewhere in these Rules, or may direct the beam of her searchlight in the direction of the danger, in such a way as not to embarrass any vessel.

DISTRESS SIGNALS

RULE 37
When a vessel is in distress and requires assistance she shall use or exhibit the signals described in Annex IV to these Regulations.

ANNEX IV

1. The following signals, used or exhibited either together or separately, indicate distress and need of assistance:

    (a)   a gun or other explosive signal fired at intervals of about a minute;

    (b)   a continuous sounding with any fog-signalling apparatus;

    (c)   rockets or shells, throwing red stars fired one at a time at short intervals;

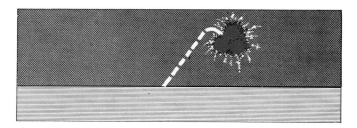

Distress rocket or shell

    (d)   a signal made by radiotelegraphy or by any other signalling method consisting of the group (SOS) in the Morse Code;

    (e)   a signal sent by radiotelephony consisting of the spoken word 'Mayday';

    (f)   the International Code Signal of distress indicated by N.C.;

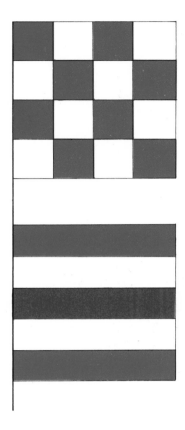

The International Code signal 'N' 'C'

(g) a signal consisting of a square flag having above or below it a ball or anything resembling a ball;

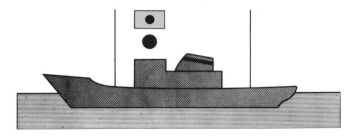

Distress signal

(h)   flames on the vessel (as from a burning tar barrel, oil barrel, etc.);

Distress signal (flames on the vessel)

(i)   a rocket parachute flare or a hand flare showing a red light;

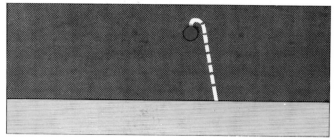

Rocket parachute flare

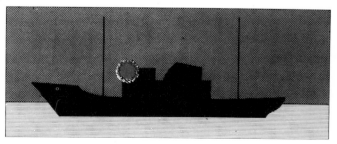

Distress signal (hand flare)

(j) a smoke signal giving off orange-coloured smoke;

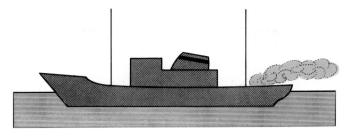

Distress signal (orange coloured smoke)

(k) slowly and repeatedly raising and lowering arms outstretched to each side;

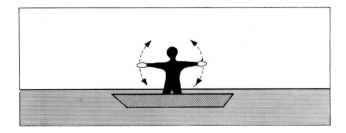

Distress signal (raising and lowering arms)

(l) the radiotelegraph alarm signal;

(m) the radiotelephone alarm signal;

(n) signals transmitted by emergency position-indicating radio beacons;

(o) approved signals transmitted by radiocommunication systems.

2. The use or exhibition of any of the foregoing signals except for the purpose of indicating distress and need of assistance and the use of other signals which may be confused with any of the above signals is prohibited.

3. Attention is drawn to the relevant sections of the International Code of Signals, the Merchant Ship Search and Rescue Manual and the following signals:

(a) a piece of orange-coloured canvas with either a black square and circle or other appropriate symbol (for identification from the air);

Distress signal (from Merchant Ship Search and Rescue Manual)

(b) a dye marker.

SECTION THREE

In this section the reader is asked to
study the lights or shapes illustrated
and to answer the following questions:

(a) What type of vessel or vessels
     would exhibit the lights or shapes
     illustrated?

(b) What sound signal is given by that
     vessel in conditions of restricted
     visibility?

(c) Assuming that any optional lights
     are not being exhibited, is the
     vessel 50 metres or more in length?

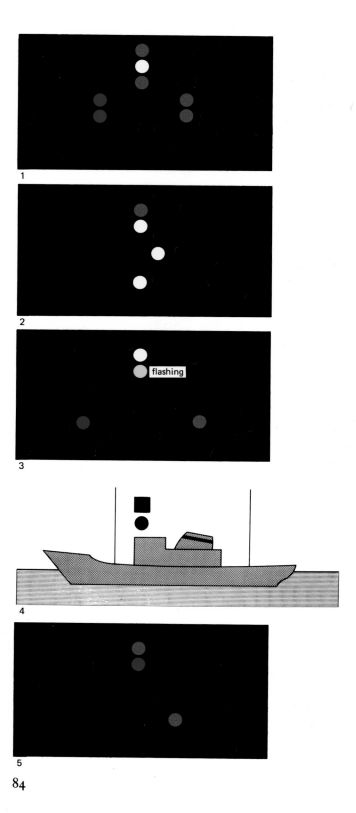

flashing

ANSWERS TO PRECEDING PAGE

1. (a) A vessel engaged in dredging, underway but not making way through the water.
   (b) One prolonged blast followed by two short blasts at intervals of not more than two minutes.
   (c) No indication of length.

2. (a) A vessel engaged in fishing other than trawling with nets extending more than 150 metres making way through the water and seen from astern.
   (b) One prolonged blast followed by two short blasts at intervals of not more than two minutes.
   (c) No indication of length.

3. (a) An air-cushion vehicle operating in the non-displacement mode seen from ahead.
   (b) One prolonged blast at intervals of not more than two minutes.
   (c) Less than 50 metres in length.

4. (a) A vessel exhibiting a distress signal.
   (b) —
   (c) —

5. (a) A sailing vessel exhibiting the optional masthead lights.
   (b) One prolonged blast followed by two short blasts at intervals of not more than two minutes.
   (c) No indication of length.

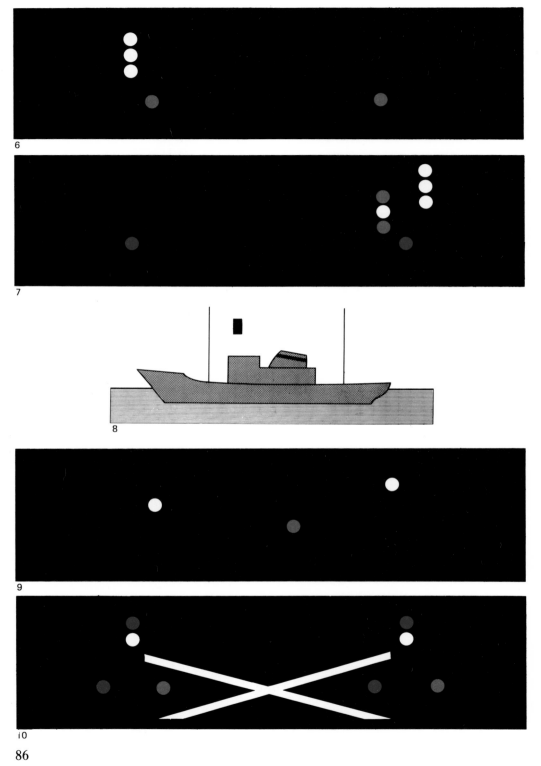

86

6. (a) A power-driven vessel engaged in towing where the length of the tow exceeds 200 metres seen from the port side.
   (b) One prolonged blast followed by two short blasts at intervals of not more than two minutes. Immediately after this the towed vessel, if manned, would sound one prolonged blast followed by three short blasts.
   (c) Less than 50 metres in length.

7. (a) A power-driven vessel engaged in towing where the length of the tow exceeds 200 metres and is unable to deviate from her course, seen from the starboard side.
   (b) One prolonged blast followed by two short blasts at intervals of not more than two minutes. Immediately after this the towed vessel, if manned, would sound one prolonged blast followed by three short blasts.
   (c) Less than 50 metres in length.

8. (a) A vessel constrained by her draught seen by day.
   (b) One prolonged blast followed by two short blasts at intervals of not more than two minutes.
   (c) No indication of length but probably more than 50 metres.

9. (a) A power-driven vessel underway and seen from the port side.
   (b) If making way through the water one prolonged blast and if stopped two prolonged blasts at intervals of not more than two minutes.
   (c) 50 metres or more in length.

10. (a) Two vessels engaged in pair trawling and using searchlights, seen from ahead and making way through the water.
   (b) One prolonged blast followed by two short blasts at intervals of not more than two minutes.
   (c) Less than 50 metres in length.

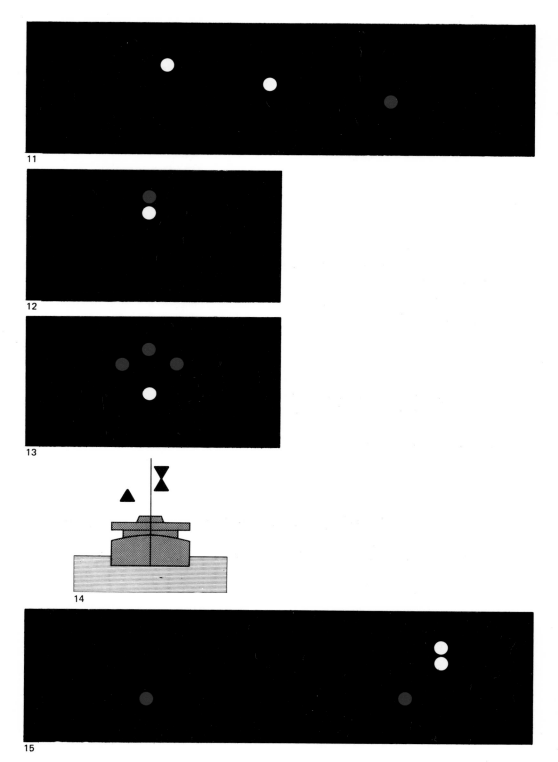

11

12

13

14

15

11. (a) Possible distribution of steaming lights for an aircraft carrier underway seen from the starboard side.
(b) If making way through the water one prolonged blast and if stopped two prolonged blasts at intervals of not more than two minutes.
(c) 50 metres or more in length.

12. (a) A vessel engaged in trawling and not making way through the water.
(b) One prolonged blast followed by two short blasts at intervals of not more than two minutes.
(c) Less than 50 metres in length.

13. (a) A vessel engaged in minesweeping and seen from astern.
(b) One prolonged blast followed by two short blasts at intervals of not more than two minutes.
(c) No indication of length.

14. (a) A vessel engaged in fishing other than trawling with nets extending more than 150 metres seen by day.
(b) One prolonged blast followed by two short blasts at intervals of not more than two minutes.
(c) 20 metres or more in length.

15. (a) A power-driven vessel engaged in towing where the length of the tow is 200 metres or less seen from the starboard side.
(b) One prolonged blast followed by two short blasts at intervals of not more than two minutes. Immediately after this the towed vessel, if manned, would sound one prolonged blast followed by three short blasts.
(c) Less than 50 metres in length.

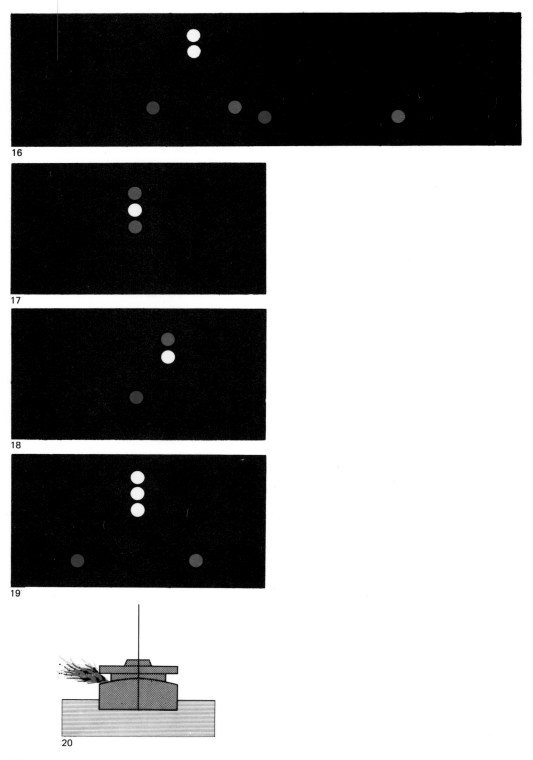

16

17

18

19

20

16. (a) A power-driven vessel engaged in towing alongside seen from ahead.
    (b) One prolonged blast followed by two short blasts at intervals of not more than two minutes.
    (c) Less than 50 metres in length.

17. (a) A vessel restricted in her ability to manoeuvre underway but not making way through the water.
    (b) One prolonged blast followed by two short blasts at intervals of not more than two minutes.
    (c) No indication of length.

18. (a) A vessel engaged in fishing other than trawling, with nets extending 150 metres or less and making way through the water, seen from the starboard side.
    (b) One prolonged blast followed by two short blasts at intervals of not more than two minutes.
    (c) No indication of length.

19. (a) A power-driven vessel of 50 metres or more in length engaged in towing where the length of the tow is 200 metres or less, seen from ahead.
    or;
    A power-driven vessel less than 50 metres in length engaged in towing where the length of the tow exceeds 200 metres, seen from ahead.
    (b) One prolonged blast followed by two short blasts at intervals of not more than two minutes. Immediately after this the towed vessel, if manned, would sound one prolonged blast followed by three short blasts.

20. (a) A signal of a vessel in distress.
    (b) —
    (c) —

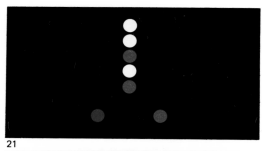

21

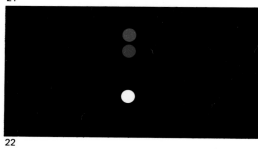

22

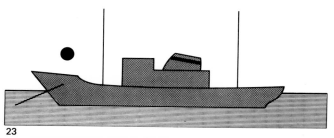

23

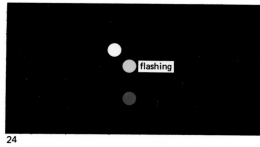

flashing

24

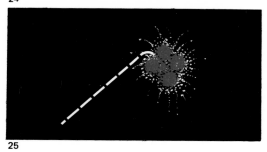

25

21. (a) A power-driven vessel restricted in her ability to manoeuvre, making way through the water and seen from ahead, or:
    A power-driven vessel engaged in towing where the length of the tow is 200 metres or less and is unable to deviate from her course, seen from ahead.
    (b) One prolonged blast followed by two short blasts at intervals of not more than two minutes in either case. However, in the latter case the towed vessel, if manned would sound, immediately after the signal from the towing vessel, one prolonged blast followed by three short blasts.
    (c) If the former, 50 metres or more in length.
    If the latter, less than 50 metres in length.

22. (a) A sailing vessel underway and exhibiting the optional masthead lights, seen from astern.
    (b) One prolonged blast followed by two short blasts at intervals of not more than two minutes.
    (c) No indication of length.

23. (a) A vessel at anchor seen by day.
    (b) A rapid ringing of the bell for about 5 seconds and, if 100 metres or more in length, followed by a rapid ringing of the gong for about 5 seconds at intervals of not more than one minute.
    (c) No indication of length.

24. (a) An air-cushion vehicle operating in the non-displacement mode and seen from the port side.
    (b) One prolonged blast at intervals of not more than two minutes.
    (c) Less than 50 metres in length.

25. (a) A signal of a vessel in distress.
    (b) —
    (c) —

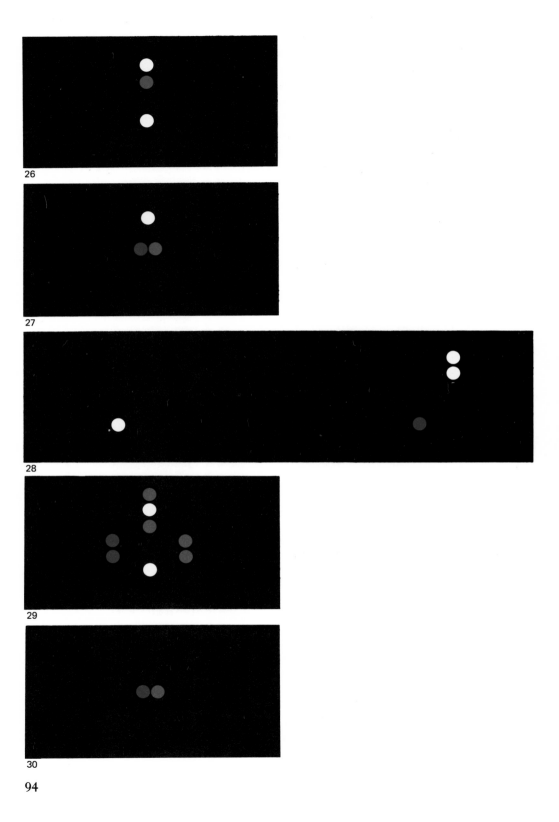

26

27

28

29

30

26. (a) A pilot vessel engaged in pilotage duty making way through the water and seen from astern, or;
A pilot vessel engaged in pilotage duty and at anchor.
(b) If the former:
One prolonged blast at intervals of not more than two minutes.
If the latter:
A rapid ringing of the bell for about 5 seconds and if 100 metres or more in length this would be followed by a rapid ringing of the gong for about 5 seconds, at intervals of not more than one minute.
Both of these fog signals may be followed by an identity signal of 4 short blasts.
(c) If the former:
No indication of length.
If the latter:
Less than 50 metres in length.

27. (a) A power-driven vessel underway and seen from ahead.
(b) If making way through the water one prolonged blast and if stopped two prolonged blasts at intervals of not more than two minutes.
(c) Less than 20 metres in length.

28. (a) A power-driven vessel engaged in towing a Dracone where the length of the tow is 200 metres or less.
(b) One prolonged blast followed by two short blasts at intervals of not more than two minutes.
(c) Less than 50 metres in length.

29. (a) A vessel engaged in dredging making way through the water and seen from astern.
(b) One prolonged blast followed by two short blasts at intervals of not more than two minutes.
(c) No indication of length.

30. (a) A sailing vessel underway and seen from ahead.
(b) One prolonged blast followed by two short blasts at intervals of not more than two minutes.
(c) Less than 20 metres in length.

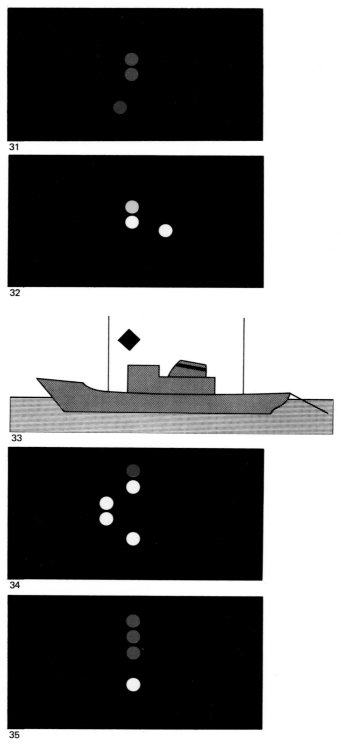

31

32

33

35

31. (a) A vessel not under command and making way through the water seen from the starboard side.
    (b) One prolonged blast followed by two short blasts at intervals of not more than two minutes.
    (c) No indication of length.

32. (a) A power-driven vessel engaged in towing seen from astern.
    (b) One prolonged blast followed by two short blasts at intervals of not more than two minutes. Immediately after this the towed vessel, if manned, would sound one prolonged blast followed by three short blasts.
    (c) No indication of length of vessel or of the length of the tow.

33. (a) A power-driven vessel engaged in towing where the length of the tow exceeds 200 metres seen by day.
    (b) One prolonged blast followed by two short blasts at intervals of not more than two minutes. Immediately after this the towed vessel, if manned, would sound one prolonged followed by three short blasts.
    (c) No indication of length.

34. (a) A vessel engaged in trawling, making way through the water and exhibiting the optional lights indicating that she is shooting her nets, seen from astern.
    (b) One prolonged blast followed by two short blasts at intervals of not more than two minutes.
    (c) No indication of length.

35. (a) A power-driven vessel constrained by her draft under way and seen from astern.
    (b) One prolonged blast followed by two short blasts at intervals of not more than two minutes.
    (c) No indication of length but probably more than 50 metres.

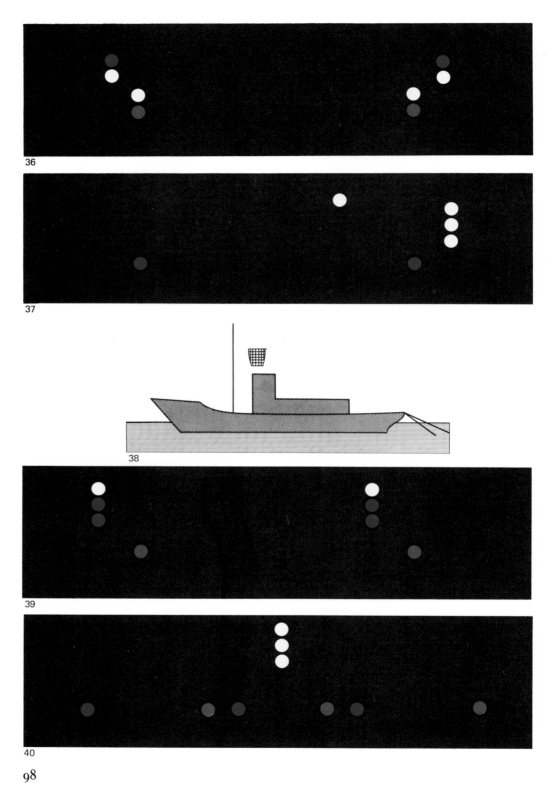

36

37

38

39

40

36. (a) Two vessels engaged in pair trawling, hauling their nets and not making way through the water.
    (b) One prolonged blast followed by two short blasts at intervals of not more than two minutes.
    (c) Less than 50 metres in length.

37. (a) A power-driven vessel engaged in towing where the length of the tow exceeds 200 metres seen from the starboard side.
    (b) One prolonged blast followed by two short blasts at intervals of not more than two minutes. Immediately after this the towed vessel, if manned, would sound one prolonged blast followed by three short blasts.
    (c) 50 metres or more in length.

38. (a) A vessel engaged in fishing seen by day.
    (b) One prolonged blast followed by two short blasts at intervals of not more than two minutes.
    (c) Less than 20 metres in length.

39. (a) Two vessels engaged in minesweeping seen from the port side.
    (b) One prolonged blast followed by two short blasts at intervals of not more than two minutes.
    (c) Less than 50 metres in length.

40. (a) A power-driven vessel engaged in towing alongside seen from ahead.
    (b) One prolonged blast followed by two short blasts at intervals of not more than two minutes.
    (c) 50 metres or more in length.

41

42

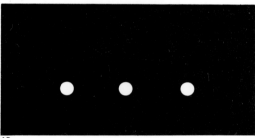

43

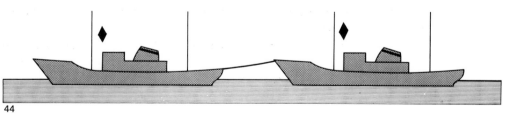

44

45

41. (a) Two vessels engaged in pair trawling making way through the water and exhibiting the optional lights indicating that they are shooting their nets.
   (b) One prolonged blast followed by two short blasts at intervals of not more than two minutes.
   (c) Less than 50 metres in length.

42. (a) A sternlight of a power-driven vessel,
   or:
   A sternlight of a sailing vessel,
   or:
   A small power-driven vessel, sailing vessel or boat under oars.

43. (a) A vessel engaged in towing alongside with a vessel on each side, as seen from astern.
   (b) One prolonged blast followed by two short blasts at intervals of not more than two minutes.
   (c) No indication of length.

44. (a) A power-driven vessel engaged in towing where the length of the tow exceeds 200 metres seen by day.
   (b) One prolonged blast followed by two short blasts at intervals of not more than two minutes. Immediately after this the towed vessel, if manned, would sound one prolonged blast followed by three short blasts.
   (c) No indication of length.

45. (a) A power-driven vessel engaged in towing where the length of the tow is 200 metres or less and is unable to deviate from her course seen from the starboard side.
   (b) One prolonged blast followed by two short blasts at intervals of not more than two minutes. Immediately after this the towed vessel, if manned, would sound one prolonged blast followed by three short blasts.
   (c) Length is less than 50 metres.

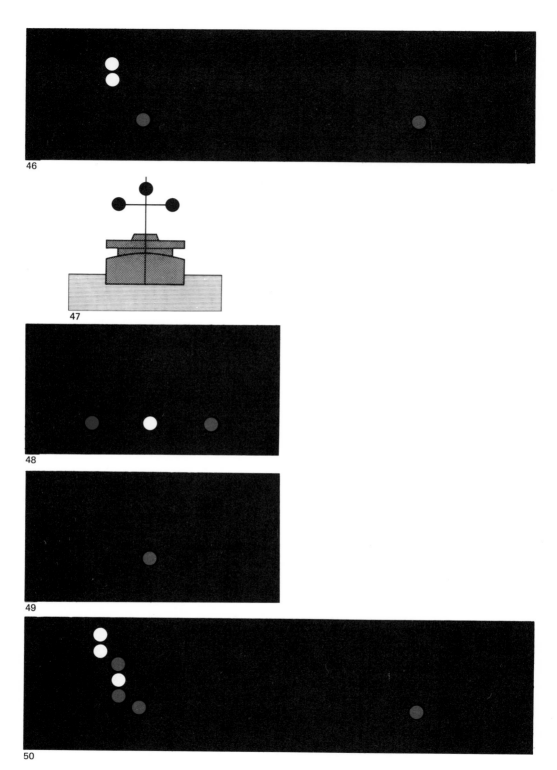

46

47

48

49

50

46. (a) A power-driven vessel engaged in towing where the length of the tow is 200 metres or less and seen from the port side.
   (b) One prolonged blast followed by two short blasts at intervals of not more than two minutes. Immediately after this the towed vessel, if manned, would sound one prolonged blast followed by three short blasts.
   (c) Less than 50 metres in length.

47. (a) A power-driven vessel engaged in minesweeping and seen by day.
   (b) One prolonged blast followed by two short blasts at intervals of not more than two minutes.
   (c) No indication of length.

48. (a) Possible distribution of a seaplanes lights while underway on the water.
   (b) If making way through the water one prolonged blast and if stopped two prolonged blasts at intervals of not more than two minutes.
   (c) Less than 50 metres in length.

49. (a) A sailing vessel underway and seen from the port side.
   (b) One prolonged blast followed by two short blasts at intervals of not more than two minutes.
   (c) No indication of length.

50. (a) A power-driven vessel engaged in towing where the length of the tow is 200 metres or less and is unable to deviate from her course seen from the port side.
   (b) One prolonged blast followed by two short blasts at intervals of not more than two minutes. Immediately after this the towed vessel, if manned, would sound one prolonged blast followed by three short blasts.
   (c) Less than 50 metres in length.

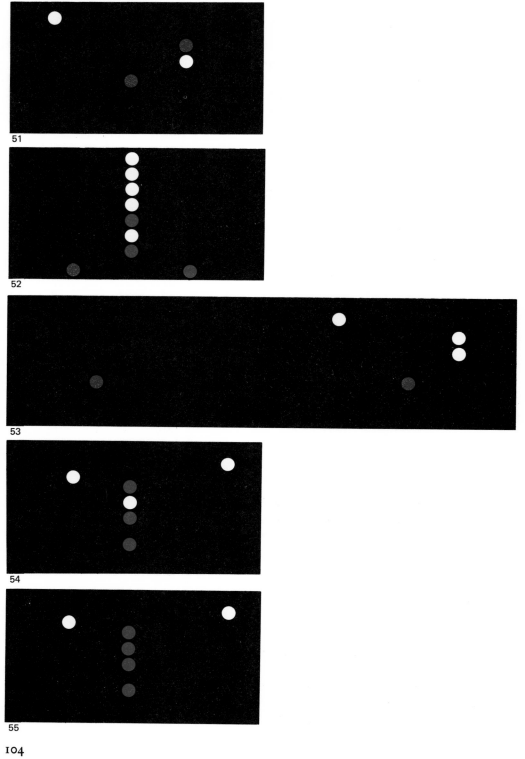

51

52

53

54

55

51. (a) A vessel engaged in trawling, making way through the water seen from the star-board side.
    (b) One prolonged blast followed by two short blasts at intervals of not more than two minutes.
    (c) 50 metres or more in length.

52. (a) A power-driven vessel engaged in towing where the length of the tow exceeds 200 metres and is unable to deviate from her course.
    (b) One prolonged blast followed by two short blasts at intervals of not more than two minutes. Immediately after this the towed vessel, if manned, would sound one prolonged blast followed by three short blasts.
    (c) 50 metres or more in length.

53. (a) A power-driven vessel engaged in towing where the length of the tow is 200 metres or less, seen from the starboard side.
    (b) One prolonged blast followed by two short blasts at intervals of not more than two minutes. Immediately after this the towed vessel, if manned, would sound one prolonged blast followed by three short blasts.
    (c) 50 metres or more in length.

54. (a) A power-driven vessel restricted in her ability to manoeuvre and making way through the water seen from the port side.
    (b) One prolonged blast followed by two short blasts at intervals of not more than two minutes.
    (c) 50 metres or more in length.

55. (a) A power-driven vessel underway and constrained by her draught seen from the port side.
    (b) One prolonged blast followed by two short blasts at intervals of not more than two minutes.
    (c) 50 metres or more in length.

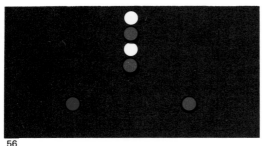

56

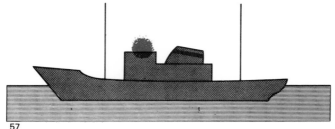

57

58

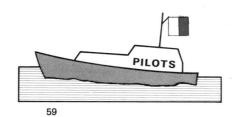

59

60

56. (a) A power-driven vessel restricted in her ability to manoeuvre making way through the water, seen from ahead.
  (b) One prolonged blast followed by two short blasts at intervals of not more than two minutes.
  (c) Less than 50 metres in length.

57. (a) A signal of a vessel in distress.
  (b) —
  (c) —

58. (a) A power-driven vessel underway and seen from ahead,
      or:
      A power-driven vessel engaged in towing where the length of the tow is 200 metres or less.
  (b) If the former;
      If making way through the water one prolonged blast and if stopped two prolonged blasts at intervals of not more than two minutes.
      If the latter;
      One prolonged blast followed by two short blasts at intervals of not more than two minutes. Immediately after this the towed vessel, if manned, would sound one prolonged blast followed by three short blasts.
  (c) If the former the length is 50 metres or more.
      If the latter the length is less than 50 metres.

59. (a) A vessel engaged on pilotage duty seen by day.
  (b) If making way through the water one prolonged blast and if stopped two prolonged blasts at intervals of not more than two minutes. In addition the vessel may sound an identity signal of 4 short blasts.
  (c) No indication of length.

60. (a) A vessel engaged on pilotage duty underway and seen from the port side.
  (b) If making way through the water one prolonged blast and if stopped two prolonged blasts at intervals of not more than two minutes. In addition the vessel may sound an identity signal of 4 short blasts.

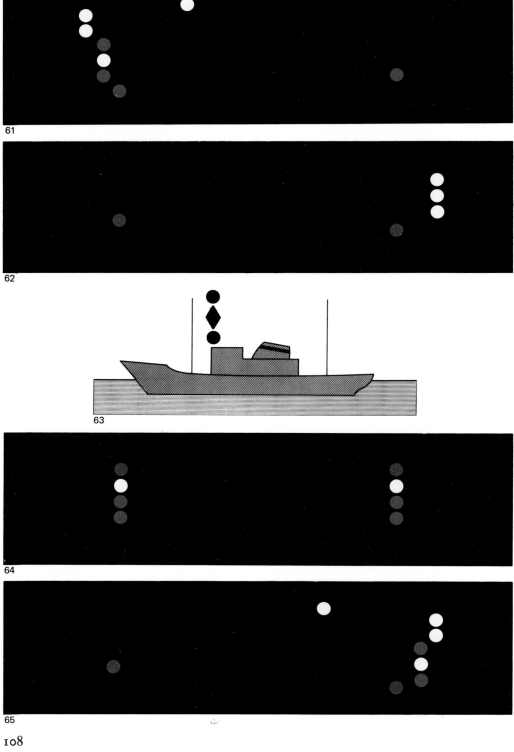

61

62

63

64

65

61. (a) A power-driven vessel engaged in towing where the length of the tow is 200 metres or less and is unable to deviate from her course, seen from the port side.
    (b) One prolonged blast followed by two short blasts at intervals of not more than two minutes. Immediately after this the towed vessel, if manned, would sound one prolonged blast followed by three short blasts.
    (c) 50 metres or more in length.

62. (a) A power-driven vessel engaged in towing where the length of the tow exceeds 200 metres and seen from the starboard side.
    (b) One prolonged blast followed by two short blasts at intervals of not more than two minutes. Immediately after this the towed vessel, if manned, would sound one prolonged blast followed by three short blasts.
    (c) Less than 50 metres in length.

63. (a) A power-driven vessel restricted in her ability to manoeuvre seen by day.
    (b) One prolonged blast followed by two short blasts at intervals of not more than two minutes.
    (c) No indication of length.

64. (a) Two vessels engaged in pair trawling with their nets fast to an obstruction and not making way through the water.
    (b) One prolonged blast followed by two short blasts at intervals of not more than two minutes.
    (c) No indication of length.

65. (a) A power-driven vessel engaged in towing where the length of the tow is 200 metres or less and is unable to deviate from her course, seen from the starboard side.
    (b) One prolonged blast followed by two short blasts at intervals of not more than two minutes. Immediately after this the towed vessel, if manned, would sound one prolonged blast followed by three short blasts.
    (c) 50 metres or more in length.

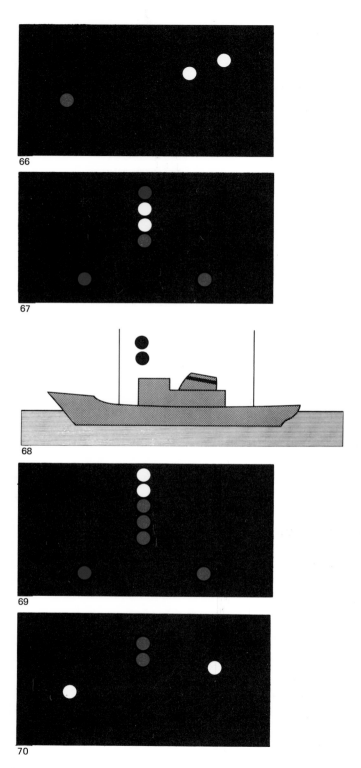

66

67

68

69

70

66. (a) Possible distribution of an aircraft carriers lights when underway and seen from the port side.
   (b) If making way through the water one prolonged blast and if stopped two prolonged blasts at intervals of not more than two minutes.
   (c) 50 metres or more in length.

67. (a) A vessel engaged in trawling and exhibiting the optional lights indicating that she is hauling her nets; making way through the water and seen from ahead.
   (b) One prolonged blast followed by two short blasts at intervals of not more than two minutes.
   (c) Less than 50 metres in length.

68. (a) A vessel not under command seen by day.
   (b) One prolonged blast followed by two short blasts at intervals of not more than two minutes.
   (c) No indication of length.

69. (a) A power-driven vessel underway and constrained by her draught and seen from ahead.
   (b) One prolonged blast followed by two short blasts at intervals of not more than two minutes.
   (c) 50 metres or more in length.

70. (a) A vessel aground.
   (b) Three strokes on the bell followed by a rapid ringing of the bell followed by three strokes on the bell and, if 100 metres or more in length follow up with a rapid ringing of the gong for about five seconds at intervals of not more than one minute. She may also give an appropriate whistle signal.
   (c) 50 metres or more in length.

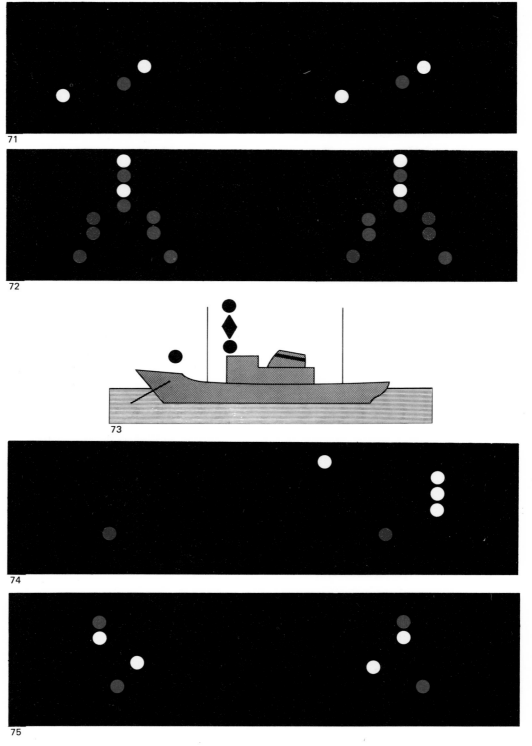

71

72

73

74

75

71. (a) Possible distribution of lights for two submarines in line astern, seen from the port side.
    (b) If making way through the water one prolonged blast and if stopped two prolonged blasts at intervals of not more than two minutes.
    (c) 50 metres or more in length.

72. (a) Two vessels engaged in dredging making way through the water and seen from ahead.
    (b) One prolonged blast followed by two short blasts at intervals of not more than two minutes.
    (c) Less than 50 metres in length.

73. (a) A vessel restricted in her ability to manoeuvre at anchor seen by day.
    (b) A rapid ringing of the bell for about 5 seconds and if 100 metres or more in length, followed by a rapid ringing of the gong at intervals of not more than one minute. In addition, she may sound a warning signal of her presence consisting of one short, one prolonged and one short blast.
    (c) No indication of length.

74. (a) A power-driven vessel engaged in towing where the length of the tow exceeds 200 metres and seen from the starboard side.
    (b) One prolonged blast followed by two short blasts at intervals of not more than two minutes. Immediately after this the towed vessel, if manned, would sound one prolonged blast followed by three short blasts.
    (c) 50 metres or more in length.

75. (a) Two vessels engaged in fishing other than trawling with nets extending more than 150 metres, making way through the water and seen from the port side.
    (b) One prolonged blast followed by two short blasts at intervals of not more than two minutes.
    (c) No indication of length.

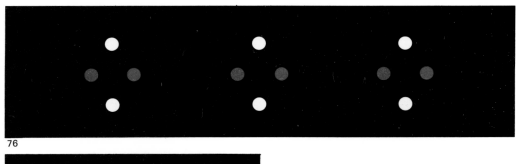

76

77

78

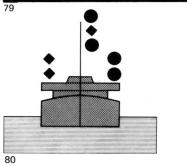

79

80

76. (a) Possible distribution of lights for three submarines underway and seen from ahead.
    (b) If making way through the water one prolonged blast and if stopped two prolonged blasts at intervals of not more than two minutes.
    (c) 50 metres or more in length.

77. (a) A sailing vessel underway seen from the starboard side.
    (b) One prolonged blast followed by two short blasts at intervals of not more than two minutes.
    (c) No indication of length.

78. (a) A vessel not under command making way through the water seen from astern, or: A vessel aground.
    (b) If the former:
        One prolonged blast followed by two short blasts at intervals of not more than two minutes.
        If the latter:
        Three strokes on the bell followed by a rapid ringing of the bell for about 5 seconds followed by three strokes on the bell; if more than 100 metres in length this would be followed by a rapid ringing of the gong for about 5 seconds, at intervals of not more than one minute. She may also give an appropriate whistle signal.
    (c) No indication of length in the case of the former and less than 50 metres in the case of the latter.

79. (a) Possible distribution of a submarines lights when underway and seen from the starboard side.
    (b) If making way through the water one prolonged blast and if stopped two prolonged blasts at intervals of not more than two minutes.
    (c) 50 metres or more in length.

80. (a) A vessel engaged in dredging seen by day.
    (b) One prolonged blast followed by two short blasts at intervals of not more than two minutes.
    (c) No indication of length.

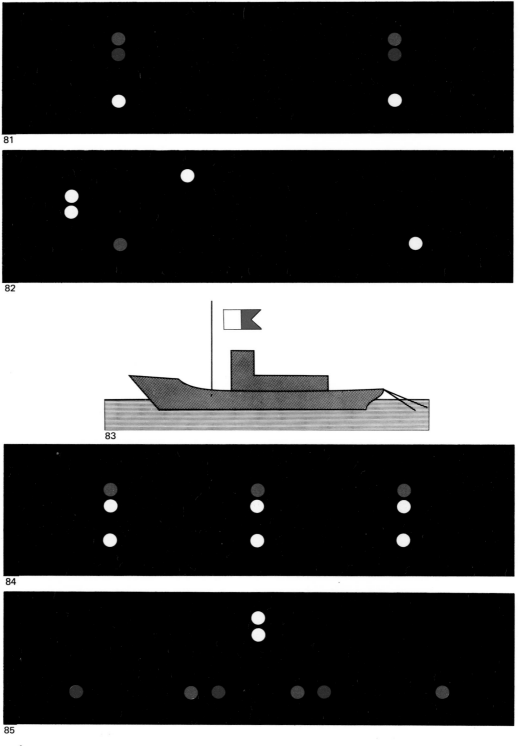

81

82

83

84

85

81. (a) Two sailing vessels underway exhibiting the optional masthead lights and seen from astern.
    (b) One prolonged blast followed by two short blasts at intervals of not more than two minutes.
    (c) No indication of length.

82. (a) A power-driven vessel engaged in towing a Dracone where the length of the tow is 200 metres or less, seen from the port side.
    (b) One prolonged blast followed by two short blasts at intervals of not more than two minutes.
    (c) 50 metres or more in length.

83. (a) A small vessel engaged in diving operations where it is impracticable to exhibit the signals for a dredger, seen by day.
    (b) One prolonged blast followed by two short blasts at intervals of not more than two minutes. However if the vessel is less than 12 metres in length she may give an efficient sound signal at intervals of not more than two minutes.
    (c) No indication of length.

84. (a) Three vessels engaged in fishing other than trawling with nets extending 150 metres or less, making way through the water and seen from astern.
    (b) One prolonged blast followed by two short blasts at intervals of not more than two minutes.
    (c) No indication of length.

85. (a) A power-driven vessel engaged in towing alongside with a vessel on each side, seen from ahead.
    (b) One prolonged blast followed by two short blasts at intervals of not more than two minutes.
    (c) Less than 50 metres in length.

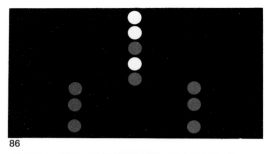

86

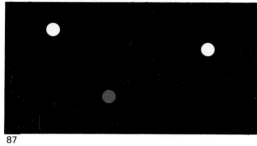

87

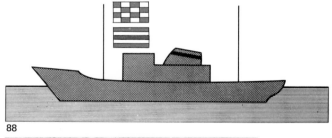

88

89

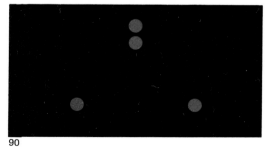

90

86. (a) A power-driven vessel engaged in dredging, making way through the water and seen from ahead.
    (b) One prolonged blast followed by two short blasts at intervals of not more than two minutes.
    (c) 50 metres or more in length.

87. (a) A power-driven vessel underway and seen from the starboard side.
    (b) If making way through the water one prolonged blast and if stopped two prolonged blasts at intervals of not more than two minutes.
    (c) 50 metres or more in length.

88. (a) A signal of a vessel in distress.
    (b) —
    (c) —

89. (a) Possible distribution of the lights for an aircraft carrier seen from ahead.
    (b) If making way through the water one prolonged blast and if stopped two prolonged blasts at intervals of not more than two minutes.
    (c) 50 metres or more in length.

90. (a) A vessel not under command making way through the water and seen from ahead.
    (b) One prolonged blast followed by two short blasts at intervals of not more than two minutes.
    (c) No indication of length.

119

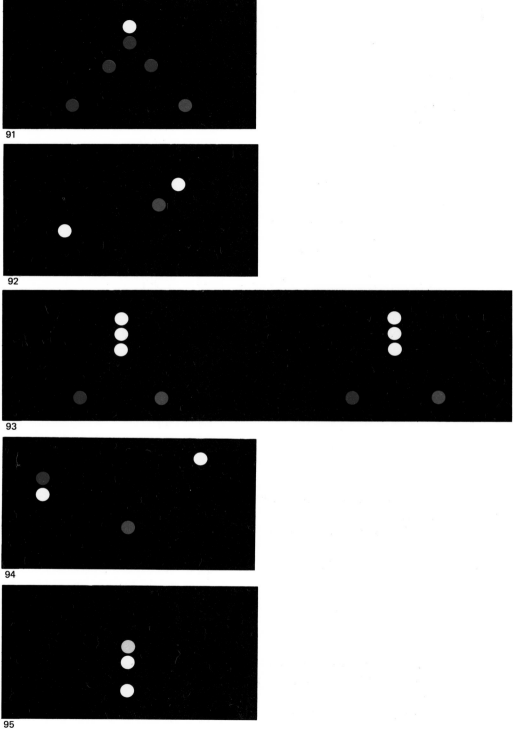

91

92

93

94

95

91. (a) A vessel engaged in mine clearance and seen from ahead.
    (b) One prolonged blast followed by two short blasts at intervals of not more than two minutes.
    (c) Less than 50 metres in length.

92. (a) Possible distribution of a submarine's lights when underway and seen from the port side.
    (b) If making way through the water one prolonged blast and if stopped two prolonged blasts at intervals of not more than two minutes.
    (c) 50 metres or more in length.

93. (a) Two power-driven vessels engaged in towing where either:
        (i) the length of the tow is 200 metres or less and the towing vessel is 50 metres or more in length, or
        (ii) the length of the tow is more than 200 metres and the length of the towing vessel is less than 50 metres.
    (b) One prolonged blast followed by two short blasts at intervals of not more than two minutes. Immediately after this the towed vessel, if manned, would sound one prolonged blast followed by three short blasts.
    (c) See (a) above.

94. (a) A vessel engaged in trawling, making way through the water and seen from the port side.
    (b) One prolonged blast followed by two short blasts at intervals of not more than two minutes.
    (c) 50 metres or more in length.

95. (a) A power-driven vessel engaged in towing seen from astern.
    (b) One prolonged blast followed by two short blasts at intervals of not more than two minutes.
    (c) No indication of length.

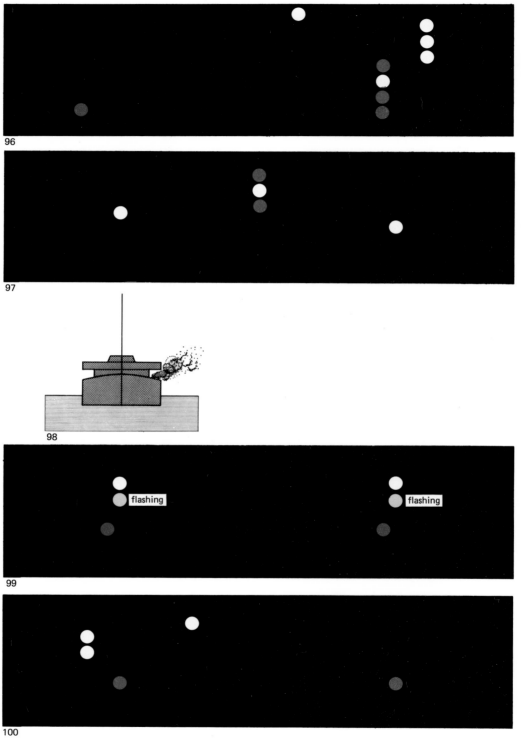

96

97

98

99

flashing   flashing

100

96. (a) A power-driven vessel engaged in towing where the length of the tow exceeds 200 metres and is unable to deviate from her course, seen from the starboard side.
   (b) One prolonged blast followed by two short blasts at intervals of not more than two minutes. Immediately after this the towed vessel, if manned, would sound one prolonged blast followed by three short blasts.
   (c) 50 metres or more in length.

97. (a) A vessel restricted in her ability to manoeuvre and at anchor.
   (b) One prolonged blast followed by two short blasts at intervals of not more than two minutes.
   (c) 50 metres or more in length.

98. (a) A signal of a vessel in distress.
   (b) —
   (c) —

99. (a) Two air-cushion vehicles operating in the non–displacement mode and seen from the starboard side.
   (b) One prolonged blast at intervals of not more than two minutes.
   (c) Less than 50 metres in length.

100. (a) A power-driven vessel engaged in towing where the length of the tow is 200 metres or less seen from the port side.
   (b) One prolonged blast followed by two short blasts at intervals of not more than two minutes. Immediately after this the towed vessel, if manned, would sound one prolonged blast followed by three short blasts.
   (c) 50 metres or more in length.

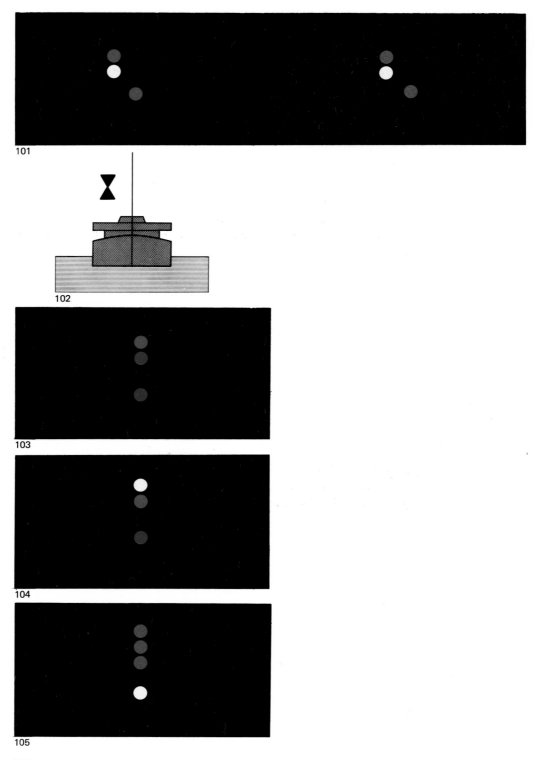

101

102

103

104

105

101. (a) Two vessels engaged in fishing other than trawling with nets extending 150 metres or less, making way and seen from the port side.
  (b) One prolonged blast followed by two short blasts at intervals of not more than two minutes.
  (c) No indication of length.

102. (a) A vessel engaged in fishing (trawling or otherwise) seen by day.
  (b) One prolonged blast followed by two short blasts at intervals of not more than two minutes.

103. (a) A sailing vessel underway exhibiting the optional masthead lights and seen from the starboard side.
  (b) One prolonged blast followed by two short blasts at intervals of not more than two minutes.
  (c) No indication of length.

104. (a) A vessel engaged on pilotage duty underway and seen from the starboard side.
  (b) If making way through the water one prolonged blast and if stopped two prolonged blasts at intervals of not more than two minutes.
  (c) No indication of length.

105. (a) A vessel constrained by her draught underway and seen from astern.
  (b) One prolonged blast followed by two short blasts at intervals of not more than two minutes.
  (c) No indication of the length.

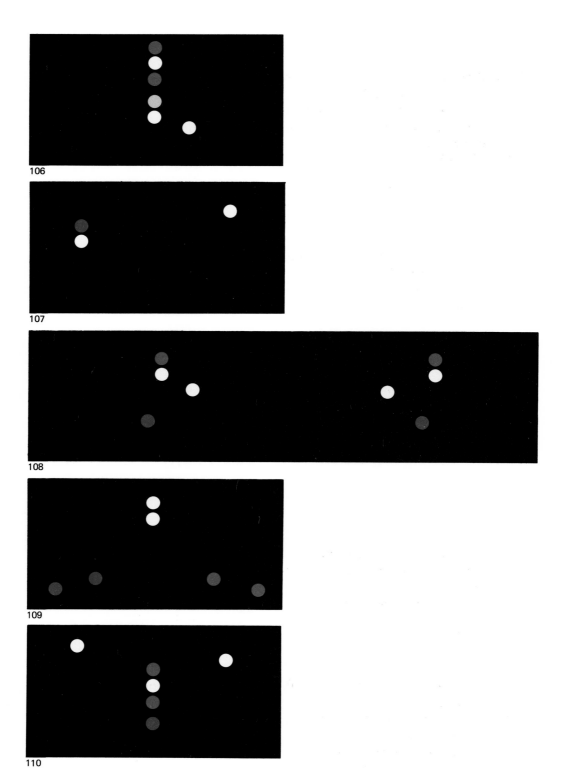

106

107

108

109

110

126

106. (a) A power-driven vessel engaged in towing where the length of the tow cannot be detected and is unable to deviate from her course, seen from astern.
  (b) One prolonged blast followed by two short blasts at intervals of not more than two minutes. Immediately after this the towed vessel, if manned, would sound one prolonged blast followed by three short blasts.
  (c) No indication of length.

107. (a) A vessel engaged in trawling not making way through the water.
  (b) One prolonged blast followed by two short blasts at intervals of not more than two minutes.
  (c) 50 metres or more in length.

108. (a) Two vessels engaged in fishing other than trawling with nets extending more than 150 metres, making way through the water and seen from the starboard side.
  (b) One prolonged blast followed by two short blasts at intervals of not more than two minutes.
  (c) No indication of length.

109. (a) A power-driven vessel engaged in pushing another vessel and seen from ahead.
  (b) One prolonged blast followed by two short blasts at intervals of not more than two minutes.
  (c) Less than 50 metres in length.

110. (a) A power-driven vessel restricted in her ability to manoeuvre, making way through the water and seen from the starboard side.
  (b) One prolonged blast followed by two short blasts at intervals of not more than two minutes.
  (c) 50 metres or more in length.

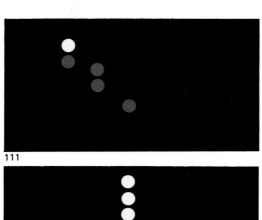

111

112

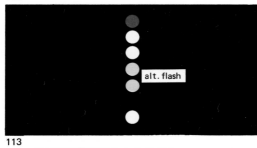

alt. flash

113

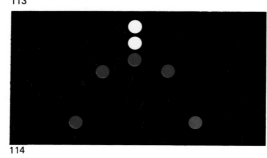

114

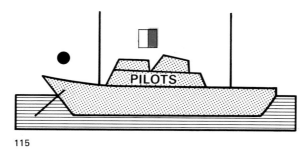

PILOTS

115

111. (a) A vessel engaged in pilotage duty not under command and making way through the water seen from the port side.
   (b) One prolonged blast followed by two short blasts at intervals of not more than two minutes.
   (c) No indication of length.

112. (a) A power-driven vessel engaged in towing where the length of the tow exceeds 200 metres, seen from ahead.
   (b) One prolonged blast followed by two short blasts at intervals of not more than two minutes. Immediately after this the towed vessel, if manned, would sound one prolonged blast followed by three short blasts.
   (c) 50 metres or more in length.

113. (a) A vessel engaged in fishing with purse seine nets and exhibiting the optional lights indicating that she is hampered by her gear. Her nets are extending more than 150 metres, making way through the water and seen from astern.
   (b) One prolonged blast followed by two short blasts at intervals of not more than two minutes.
   (c) No indication of length.

114. (a) A vessel engaged in mine clearance and seen from ahead.
   (b) One prolonged blast followed by two short blasts at intervals of not more than two minutes.
   (c) 50 metres or more in length.

115. (a) A vessel engaged in pilotage duty at anchor seen by day.
   (b) A rapid ringing of the bell for about 5 seconds and if 100 metres or more in length followed by a rapid ringing of the gong for about 5 seconds at intervals of not more than one minute.
   (c) No indication of length.

116

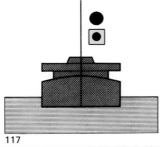

117

118

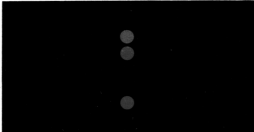

119

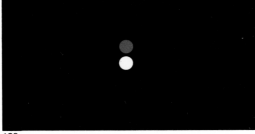

120

116. (a) Two vessels engaged in fishing with purse seine gear with nets extending more than 150 metres, exhibiting the optional lights indicating that they are hampered by their gear, making way through the water and seen from astern.
(b) One prolonged blast followed by two short blasts at intervals of not more than two minutes.
(c) No indication of length.

117. (a) A signal of a vessel in distress.
(b) —
(c) —

118. (a) A vessel engaged in trawling exhibiting the optional lights indicating that her net is fast to an obstruction and not making way through the water.
(b) One prolonged blast followed by two short blasts at intervals of not more than two minutes.
(c) No indication of length.

119. (a) A sailing vessel underway exhibiting the optional masthead lights and seen from the starboard side.
(b) One prolonged blast followed by two short blasts at intervals of not more than two minutes.
(c) No indication of length.

120. (a) A vessel engaged in fishing with nets extending 150 metres or less either underway and not making way through the water or at anchor.
(b) One prolonged blast followed by two short blasts at intervals of not more than two minutes.
(c) No indication of length.

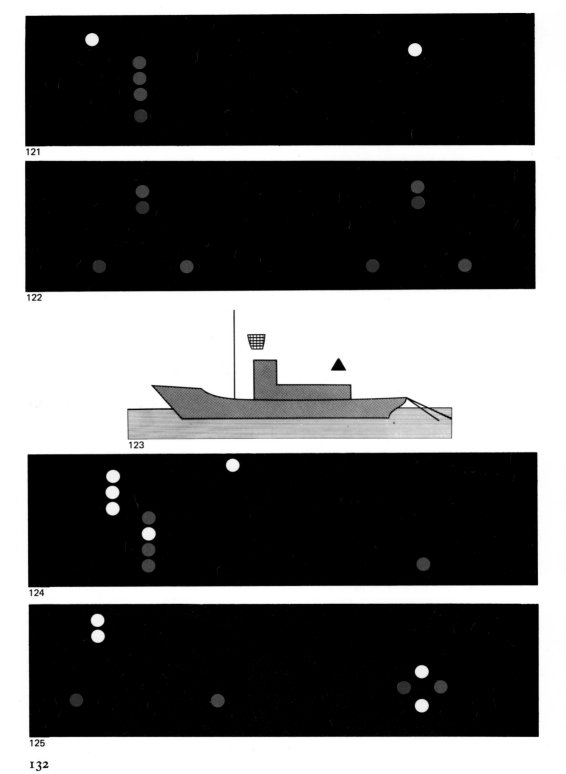

121

122

123

124

125

121. (a) A power-driven vessel underway and constrained by her draught seen from the starboard side.
   (b) If making way through the water one prolonged blast and if stopped two prolonged blasts at intervals of not more than two minutes.
   (c) 50 metres or more in length.

122. (a) Two sailing vessels underway and showing the optional masthead lights, seen from ahead.
   (b) One prolonged blast followed by two short blasts at intervals of not more than two minutes.
   (c) No indication of length.

123. (a) A vessel engaged in fishing other than trawling with nets extending more than 150 metres, seen by day.
   (b) One prolonged blast followed by two short blasts at intervals of not more than two minutes.
   (c) Less than 20 metres in length.

124. (a) A power-driven vessel engaged in towing where the length of the tow exceeds 200 metres and is unable to deviate from her course, seen from the port side.
   (b) One prolonged blast followed by two short blasts at intervals of not more than two minutes. Immediately after this the towed vessel, if manned, would sound one prolonged blast followed by three short blasts.
   (c) 50 metres or more in length.

125. (a) Possible distribution of lights for an aircraft carrier and submarine in company, seen from ahead.
   (b) If making way through the water one prolonged blast and if stopped two prolonged blasts at intervals of not more than two minutes.
   (c) In both cases 50 metres or more in length.

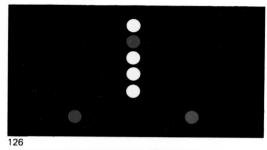

126

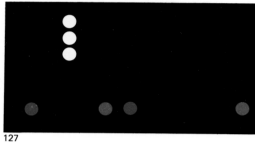

127

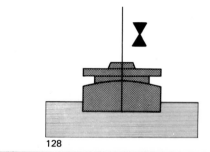

128

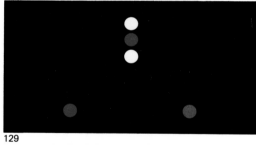

129

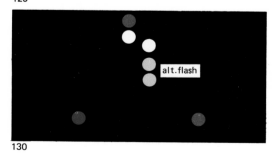

alt.flash

130

126. (a) A vessel engaged in trawling and exhibiting the optional lights indicating that she is shooting her nets, making way through the water and seen from ahead.
   (b) One prolonged blast followed by two short blasts at intervals of not more than two minutes.
   (c) 50 metres or more in length.

127. (a) A power-driven vessel engaged in towing alongside with one vessel on her port side, seen from ahead.
   (b) One prolonged blast followed by two short blasts at intervals of not more than two minutes.
   (c) 50 metres or more in length.

128. (a) A vessel engaged in fishing (if net fishing then the nets extend 150 metres or less) seen by day.
   (b) One prolonged blast followed by two short blasts at intervals of not more than two minutes.
   (c) 20 metres or more in length.

129. (a) A vessel engaged in trawling and making way through the water seen from ahead.
   (b) One prolonged blast followed by two short blasts at intervals of not more than two minutes.
   (c) 50 metres or more in length.

130. (a) A vessel engaged in fishing with purse seine gear and with nets extending more than 150 metres, making way through the water and seen from ahead. (The alternate flashing yellow lights are optional)
   (b) One prolonged blast followed by two short blasts at intervals of not more than two minutes.
   (c) No indication of length.

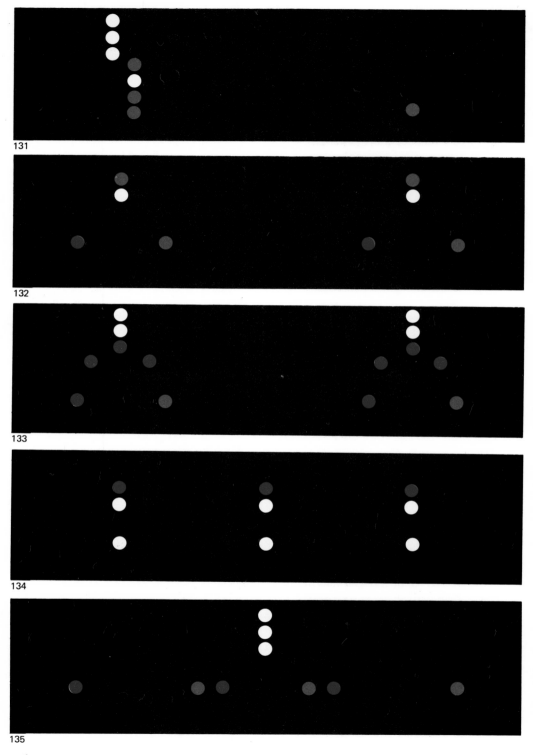

131

132

133

134

135

131. (a) A power-driven vessel engaged in towing where the length of the tow exceeds 200 metres and is unable to deviate from her course, seen from the port side.
    (b) One prolonged blast followed by two short blasts at intervals of not more than two minutes. Immediately after this the towed vessel, if manned, would sound one prolonged blast followed by three short blasts.
    (c) Less than 50 metres in length.

132. (a) Two vessels engaged in fishing other than trawling with nets extending 150 metres or less making way through the water and seen from ahead.
    (b) One prolonged blast followed by two short blasts at intervals of not more than two minutes.
    (c) No indication of length.

133. (a) Two power-driven vessels engaged in mine clearance and seen from ahead.
    (b) One prolonged blast followed by two short blasts at intervals of not more than two minutes.
    (c) 50 metres or more in length.

134. (a) Three vessels engaged in trawling, making way through the water and seen from astern.
    (b) One prolonged blast followed by two short blasts at intervals of not more than two minutes.
    (c) No indication of length.

135. (a) A power-driven vessel engaged in towing alongside with a vessel on each side seen from ahead.
    (b) One prolonged blast followed by two short blasts at intervals of not more than two minutes.
    (c) 50 metres or more in length.

137

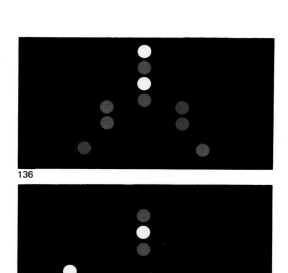

136

137

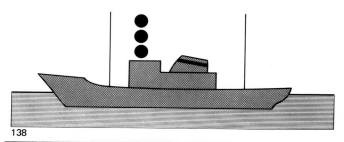

138

139

140

136. (a) A vessel engaged in dredging, making way through the water and seen from ahead.
  (b) One prolonged blast followed by two short blasts at intervals of not more than two minutes.
  (c) Less than 50 metres in length.

137. (a) A vessel restricted in her ability to manoeuvre, at anchor.
  (b) One prolonged blast followed by two short blasts at intervals of not more than two minutes.
  (c) Less than 50 metres in length.

138. (a) A vessel aground seen by day.
  (b) Three strokes on the bell followed by a rapid ringing of the bell for about 5 seconds again followed by three strokes on the bell and, if 100 metres or more in length, a rapid ringing of the gong for about 5 seconds at intervals of not more than one minute. She may also give an appropriate whistle signal.
  (c) No indication of length.

139. (a) A vessel engaged on pilotage duty at anchor.
  (b) A rapid ringing of the bell for about 5 seconds and, if 100 metres or more in length, a rapid ringing of the gong for about 5 seconds at intervals of not more than one minute. She may also sound an identity signal consisting of four short blasts.
  (c) 50 metres or more in length.

140. (a) A power-driven vessel restricted in her ability to manoeuvre, making way through the water seen from ahead;
    or:
    A power-driven vessel engaged in towing where the length of the tow is 200 metres or less and is unable to deviate from her course, seen from ahead.
  (b) One prolonged blast followed by two short blasts at intervals of not more than two minutes. In the latter case immediately after this the towed vessel, if manned, would sound one prolonged blast followed by three short blasts.
  (c) If the former 50 metres or more in length.
    If the latter less than 50 metres in length.

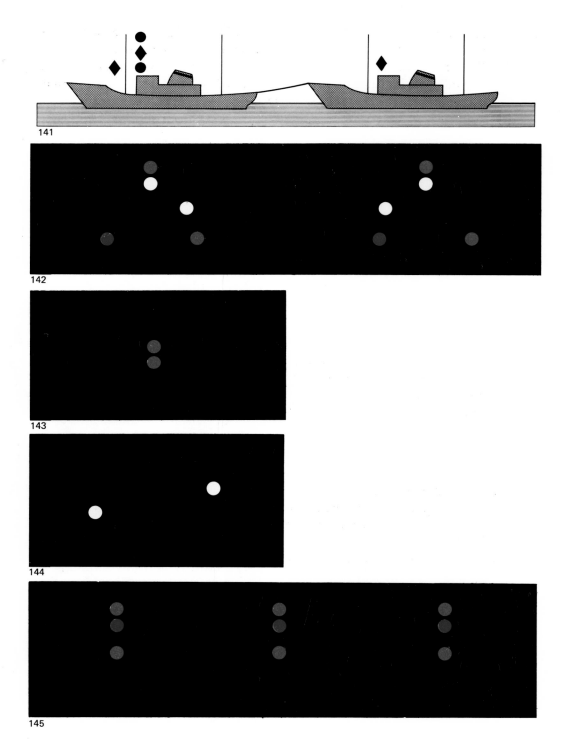

141

142

143

144

145

141. (a) A power-driven vessel engaged in towing where the length of the tow exceeds 200 metres and is unable to deviate from her course seen by day.
 (b) One prolonged blast followed by two short blasts at intervals of not more than two minutes. Immediately after this the towed vessel, if manned, would sound one prolonged blast followed by three short blasts.
 (c) No indication of length.

142. (a) Two vessels engaged in fishing other than trawling with nets extending more than 150 metres, making way through the water and seen from ahead.
 (b) One prolonged blast followed by two short blasts at intervals of not more than two minutes.
 (c) No indication of length.

143. (a) A vessel not under command and not making way through the water.
 (b) One prolonged blast followed by two short blasts at intervals of not more than two minutes.
 (c) No indication of length.

144. (a) A vessel at anchor.
 (b) A rapid ringing of the bell for about 5 seconds and, if 100 metres or more in length, followed by a rapid ringing of the gong for about 5 seconds at intervals of not more than one minute. She may also give an appropriate whistle signal.
 (c) 50 metres or more in length.

145. (a) A group of sailing vessels exhibiting the optional masthead lights and seen from the port side.
 (b) One prolonged blast followed by two short blasts at intervals of not more than two minutes.
 (c) No indication of length.